Financial Innovations

Financial Innovations

Their Impact on Monetary Policy and Financial Markets

The Federal Reserve Bank of St. Louis

Springer-Science+Business Media, B. V.

Distributors for North America:
KLUWER ACADEMIC PUBLISHERS, BOSTON
190 Old Derby Street
Hingham, MA 02043, U.S.A.

Distributors Outside North America:
Kluwer Academic Publishers Group
Distribution Centre
P.O. Box 322
3300AH Dordrecht, The Netherlands

Library of Congress Cataloging in Publication Data
Main entry under title:

Financial innovations.

Papers from the seventh annual economic conference held Oct. 1-2, 1982.
Contents: Microeconomic and macroeconomic origins of financial innovation / Edward J. Kane—Financial innovations and financial instability / Hyman P. Minsky / Discussion by Allan H. Meltzer—[etc.]
1. Finance—United States—Congresses. 2. Monetary policy—United States—Congresses. 3. Money supply—United States—Congresses. Federal Reserve Bank of St. Louis.

HG181.F625 1984 332'.0973 83-22216

ISBN 978-94-017-5372-2 ISBN 978-94-017-5370-8 (eBook)
DOI 10.1007/978-94-017-5370-8

Originally published by Kluwer Nijhoff Publishing in 1984
Softcover reprint of the hardcover 1st edition 1984

Contents

Contributing Authors

Michael J. Hamburger, Consultant, Office of Management and Budget, Old Executive Office Building, Room 244, Washington, DC 20551

Scott E. Hein, Professor of Finance, Texas Tech University, Lubbock, Texas 79409

Donald D. Hester, Professor of Economics, Social Science Building, University of Wisconsin, Madison, WI 53706

Jerry L. Jordan, Professor of Financial Management, Anderson Schools of Management, University of New Mexico, Albuquerque, NM 87131

Edward J. Kane, Professor of Economics, Ohio State University, 1775 College Road, Columbus, OH 43210

Allan H. Meltzer, Professor of Political Economy and Public Policy, Carnegie-Mellon University, Graduate School of Industrial Administration, Schenley Park, Pittsburgh, PA 15213

Laurence H. Meyer, Chairman, Economics Department, Washington University, P.O. Box 1208, St. Louis, MO 63130

Hyman P. Minsky, Professor of Economics, Washington University, St. Louis, MO 63130

Edward K. Offenbacher, Visiting Economist, Bank of Israel, Kiryat Ben-Gurion, Jerusalem 91007, Israel

Richard D. Porter, Chief, Econometric and Computer Applications Section, Division of Research and Statistics, Board of Governors of the Federal Reserve System, 20th Street and Constitution Avenue, N.W., Washington, DC 20551

Lawrence K. Roos, Special Limited Partner, Bear, Stearns and Company, 11433 Olde Cabin Lane, Suite 301, St. Louis, MO 63141

J. Richard Zecher, Senior Vice President and Chief Economist, The Chase Manhattan Bank, N.A., One Chase Manhattan Plaza, New York, NY 10081

PREFACE

On October 1 and 2, 1982, the Federal Reserve Bank of St. Louis hosted its seventh annual economic policy conference, "Financial Innovations: Their Impact on Monetary Policy and Financial Markets." This book contains the papers and discussions presented at the conference.

The process of financial innovation and its impact are highly controversial and widely debated. Opinions differ as to whether innovations have contributed to or actually impaired the efficiency and stability of financial markets. There is similar disagreement as to whether innovations have distorted the nature and meaning of the monetary aggregates, rendering them useless as intermediate targets for monetary policy. The purpose of this conference was to examine these areas of contention in order to provide a clearer understanding of the research that has been done and the areas that remain to be investigated.

The papers in Part I focus on the origins of financial innovation and their consequences for the stability of the financial system. Part II contains papers that examine the empirical impact of innovation on the measurement of money and the use of monetary targets in conducting policy. In Part III, the papers assess the broader impact of innovation on the conduct of policy and financial risk management. Finally, Part IV contains the luncheon address given at this conference by Lawrence K. Roos, then president of the Federal Reserve Bank of St. Louis.

In the first paper in Part I, "Microeconomic and Macroeconomic Origins of Financial Innovations," Edward J. Kane, the Everett D. Reese professor of banking and monetary economics at Ohio State University, compares the process of financial innovation to that of the shape-shifting that appears in myths and legends. He argues that innovations represent deliberate, albeit unintended, economic responses to macroeconomic and regulatory policies. Viewing the burdens imposed on financial firms by policy as implicit taxes, he suggests that innovations are the outcome of a regulatory dialectic process: firms respond to the regulatory-imposed burdens by innovating to minimize the burdens, and regulators respond to the induced innovations by changing the regulations to regain control over the firms. Further, exogenous and induced-endogenous factors contribute to the process and the evolving innovations. Among these factors are technology and market forces that provide further incentives and opportunities for innovation by directly confronting existing regulatory structure.

In "Financial Innovations and Financial Instability: Observations and Theory," Hyman P. Minsky, professor of economics at Washington University, St. Louis, assesses the impact of financial innovations within the context of his financial instability hypothesis. This hypothesis holds that capitalist economies are subject to business cycles and, under certain circumstances, threats of runaway inflation or deep depression. Minsky examines the impact of innovations on capital asset prices, investment, profits, and the sensitivity of the financial system to interest rate movements.

Minsky argues that innovations have compounded the problems faced by financial markets and, in particular, by the Federal Reserve. Specifically, because the Federal Reserve must serve as a lender of last resort in the face of financial crunches, it necessarily abandons its responsibility for regulating the pace of monetary growth. In Minsky's view, the Federal Reserve has no effective control over its liabilities during the period that it functions as a lender of last resort. Moreover, Minsky concludes, since innovations have increased the amount of financing available from any given reserve base, and since they have created instruments that function as money, the Federal Reserve cannot control the money supply.

In his discussion of Minsky's paper, Allan H. Meltzer, professor of political economy and public policy at Carnegie-Mellon University, addresses two issues about which he disagrees with Minsky. First, Minsky argues that the Federal Reserve cannot control the money stock and serve as a lender of last resort. Meltzer points out that this is incorrect. The lender of last resort, by increasing the monetary base to offset currency drains and other factors that would sharply reduce the money multiplier, *maintains* control of the money stock. Second, Meltzer argues that there is no merit to Minsky's recommendation that banks be permitted to hold equities unless the rates on deposit insurance that they pay reflect the additional risks that banks incur by increasing the real assets they hold. If deposit insurance rates do not adjust to reflect the additional risk, banks will be encouraged to underestimate the risks they accept. Finally, Meltzer notes that, despite Minsky's view that innovations have added to the instability of the financial system and, presumably, the aggregate economy as well, the past 25 years represent a historically stable period in U.S. history, whether viewed from the behavior of velocity or real output growth.

In the first paper in Part II, "Financial Innovations and the Measurement of Monetary Aggregates," Richard D. Porter, chief of the econometric and computer applications section, Board of Governors of the Federal Reserve System, and Edward K. Offenbacher, visiting scholar at the Bank of Israel, note that estimates of the standard narrow money demand functions have broken down since the mid-1970s and that financial innovations have been widely cited as a major cause of the money demand shifts. They investigate the impact of financial innovations on money demand in two different ways. First, they suggest that some innovations have lowered the real transaction costs associated with using money; using a Miller-Orr transaction model to derive a transaction demand for the demand deposit component of money, they show that money-demand simulations using several measures of brokerage fees are considerably better than those generated by the standard transaction equation for demand deposits.

Porter and Offenbacher then investigate the impact of financial innovations that have increased the variety of financial assets with some monetary attributes. They note that such assets function both as money and as a store of value in varying proportions. They calculate divisia monetary aggregates, which attempt to separate the monetary services from pure store-of-value functions for financial assets and aggregate the total of monetary services across these assets. Their results indicate that, using M1 alone, simple sum aggregation provides the most useful formulation for money demand (using the Porter-Simpson money demand specification). When broader aggregates are considered, however, the divisia aggregates provide the best overall results of any aggregate and any specification.

In his comment on the Porter-Offenbacher paper, Scott E. Hein, then a senior economist at the Federal Reserve Bank of St. Louis, argues that their results do not adequately explain the mid-1970s' breakdown in the conventional money-demand relationships. Hein notes that, although the brokerage-free aspects of financial innovations may *theoretically* shed some light on what might be affecting money demand, Porter-Offenbacher's empirical estimation and use of brokerage fees in their analysis is deficient. Hein shows that the first proxy that Porter-Offenbacher use to explain shifts in money demand is, in fact, derived from the posited shifts themselves; the results appear to be based more on definitional circularity than causality. Hein then points out that Porter-Offenbacher's second proxy for brokerage fees yields empirical results that are inconsistent with the underlying Miller-Orr model.

In discussing Porter-Offenbacher's analysis of the divisia aggregates, Hein notes that the superiority of divisia aggregation is potentially useful only if broader aggregates than M1 are considered; Porter-Offenbacher, he argues, provide no discussion as to why policymakers should focus on the broader monetary aggregates. Moreover, divisia aggregation for policy purposes involves predicting interest rate differentials for the included aggregates, something that is notoriously difficult to do. Hence, achieving a divisia aggregate target would appear to involve problems that remain, as yet, unsolved.

In "Financial Innovation and Monetary Targeting," Michael J. Hamburger, consultant for the Office of Management and Budget, assesses the impact of innovation via two different routes. First, he updates and analyzes the money-demand equation that he had previously published to see whether innovations produced breakdowns in it similar to those cited in standard money-demand equations. Hamburger's equation differs from conventional ones in that it excludes short-term interest rates, but includes longer-term interest yields and the dividend-price ratio on common stocks as measures of the opportunity cost of holding money. He finds that his money-demand equation, transformed into a velocity equation, does not break down in recent years.

He then assesses the characteristics of M1 velocity independent of any constraints imposed by a specific money-demand formulation. He finds that, if anything, the relationship between M1 and GNP was more stable in the 1970s than in the 1954–1970 period.

In his subsequent discussion, Laurence H. Meyer, chairman of the economics department at Washington University, points out that Hamburger's results demonstrate that there are two problems to be solved: Why does the conventional money-demand specification break down after 1973? and Why doesn't Hamburger's specification break down?

First, he notes that Hamburger's specification, which incorporates both an income elasticity of money demand equal to unity and long-term rates, runs counter to what the data in the sample period would suggest. Moreover,

Meyer points out that Hamburger's analysis, in his view, yields conflicting claims. If, as Hamburger suggests, the discrepancy between the results of his equation and the usual money-demand specification results from a dramatic decline in real transaction costs associated with holding short-term financial assets, velocity growth since 1973 should have been noticeably affected. Although Hamburger does not find this to have occurred, Meyer shows that estimation of the interest rate term structure yields a shift consistent with Hamburger's view of decline in transaction costs in the post-1973 period. Meyer then argues that Hamburger is incorrect when he concludes that velocity growth remains essentially unchanged since 1973. He presents evidence that velocity growth has risen over this period.

In the first paper in Part III, Jerry L. Jordan, professor of financial management at the Anderson Schools of Management, University of New Mexico, and former member of President Reagan's Council of Economic Advisers, discusses "Financial Innovation and Monetary Policy." In his view, financial innovations have had some impact—for example, the redefinition of M1—but have not made the use of reserve or monetary aggregate targeting obsolete, nor have they significantly reduced the usefulness of M1 as the most reliable indicator of policy actions on the economy. He contends that the debate over financial innovations, however, has served to reduce the credibility of monetary policymakers. In part, this has occurred because policymakers have sought to explain away the discrepancies between their announced target ranges and actual money growth by ad hoc reference to the impact of innovations; in part, their credibility has been strained by their increased emphasis on broader monetary or credit aggregates that they cannot control.

In "Financial Innovations in the 1980s," J. Richard Zecher, senior vice-president, Chase Manhattan Bank, explains how substantial innovations always change the opportunities available to investors. In his view, the major factors that have brought significant change in the last decade are the changes in the domestic and international monetary regimes. As a result of these changes, inflation, interest rates, and exchange rates have become more volatile, rendering many financial regulations obsolete and providing incentives for innovative financial market activity. Zecher sees this trend continuing in the 1980s.

Donald D. Hester, professor of economics at the University of Wisconsin-Madison, disagrees with Zecher's argument that the innovations by financial firms over the past 15 years have greatly lowered the costs of managing financial services and risk; Hester notes that the low earnings and stock prices of banks and other financial firms did not conform to this view. Similarly, he points out that many important innovations predated the changes in domestic and international monetary regimes that Zecher claims provided the impetus for innovations.

In his luncheon address to the conference, found in Part IV, Lawrence K. Roos, former president of the Federal Reserve Bank of St. Louis, points out that the controversy over the impact of financial innovation posed some fundamental problems for policymakers. If innovations have significantly distorted key relationships, either between Federal Reserve actions and the money stock or between the money stock and aggregate economic activity, then policymakers must find new indicators and new targets for policy. On the other hand, if the key relationships have not been distorted by innovations, then monetary aggregate targeting remains both useful and appropriate.

Roos then assesses the impact of innovations on the three navigational concepts that he uses to guide his policy decisions: (1) inflation is a monetary phenomenon; (2) abrupt and substantial changes in the growth of money can have dramatic and usually unfortunate consequences on the economy; and (3) money growth can be controlled by controlling the growth of the monetary base. Viewing the events over the past three years, he notes that these concepts still seem to provide useful and validated explanations of what actually occurred. He concludes that, whatever impact innovations may have had, they did not seriously affect the usefulness of monetary targeting for policy purposes.

I ORIGINS OF FINANCIAL INNOVATION AND THE CONSEQUENCES ON THE STABILITY OF THE FINANCIAL SYSTEM

1 MICROECONOMIC AND MACROECONOMIC ORIGINS OF FINANCIAL INNOVATION

Edward J. Kane

Shape-shifting is a central concept in literatures as diverse as modern science fiction and ancient Indian legend. Shape-shifters change their species and functional capabilities as easily as you or I change our clothes. The rock song "Vital Signs" by Rush goes so far as to depict shape-shifting as everyday behavior.

> Everybody got mixed feelings
> About the function and the form.
> Everybody got to elevate from the norm.[1]

In recent years, institutional shape-shifting has become the key to success in the world of retail finance. Some mutual funds have made their product nearly indistinguishable from bank and thrift deposits. In turn, sweep arrangements have made bank and thrift deposits increasingly less distinguishable from money market instruments. On a more cosmic level, robotization and electronification of systems for delivering financial services

---

Opinions expressed are those of the author and not those of the National Bureau of Economic Research. The author is grateful to Frank Steindl for criticism of an earlier draft.

are transforming banks into cash managers, brokers into banks, wholesale financial firms into retail ones, and absorbing local and regional financial firms into national and international conglomerates.

Shape-shifting by financial firms goes by the more prosaic name of financial innovation. Mainstream macroeconomic models treat financial innovation as an autonomous development. In typical models of the national economy, financial change is accounted for only after the fact, by testing and affirming hypotheses about dummy-variable shifts in parametric structure or in the unobservable distribution of stochastic errors. This approach assumes implicitly that financial change cannot or need not be explained by the economic forces featured in the model.

For purposes of successful monetary and regulatory policymaking, this way of thinking is dangerously flawed. Attempts to control the financial system—whether for macroeconomic or microeconomic ends—force institutions and markets to alter their shapes in important and broadly predictable ways. If policymakers do not incorporate policy-induced innovation into their ex ante planning framework, their efforts at control will be biased toward shortfall. This proposition has the force of a mathematical theorem.

In recent U.S. history, one can see wide application for this pseudo-theorem. Since inflation sharply accelerated in 1965, U.S. policies for monetary control and deposit institution regulation repeatedly have fallen short of their stated goals. Although political pressures often lead authorities to promise more than they reasonably expect to deliver, it is hard to believe that the extravagance of political promises explains more than a part of the story. Public statements by representatives of the Federal Reserve and other federal regulatory agencies express genuine surprise at the efficiency with which financial markets and institutions were able to adapt themselves to minimize the burdens that macroeconomic and regulatory policies sought, for the common good, to foist on them.

The Regulatory Dialectic

My writings on this subject put forward a dynamic model which views intended policy burdens as implicit taxes, which any burdened party (or regulatee) must be expected to seek to avoid. Moreover, even persons and institutions that are not directly burdened by a particular policy are expected to be alert to opportunities for profit opened up by regulatees' search for additional avoidance options. In principle, a regulatee should undertake avoidance activity until he or she reaches the point where the marginal costs of further avoidance equals the marginal benefit (or implicit tax rate). Underestimating the efficiency of avoidance activity means overestimating the marginal cost to regulatees of rearranging their accounts and introduces a continual need for authorities—after a lag for recognition and response—to redesign and recalibrate their policies to beat back the unintended effects of regulatee avoidance.

Recognizing that regulatees are active rather than passive taxpayers leads to an evolutionary perspective on monetary and deposit institution regulatory policies that I call the *regulatory dialectic* [Kane, 1977, 1981]. This model portrays financial change as the outcome of a continuing struggle between opposing economic and political forces. In figure 1-1, the forces the model interprets are depicted schematically as the sides and diagonal of a rectangle. Exogenous to the model are technological change (i.e., the invention of new ways of performing financial services) and the outcome of political processes that designate regulatory and monetary-policy objectives. Endogenous to the model is adaptive interaction between political and economic pressures in

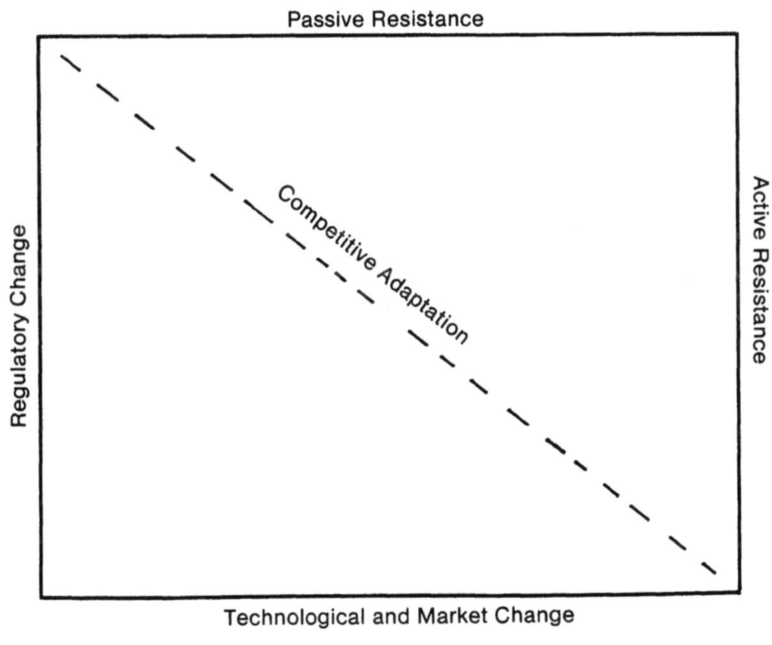

Figure 1-1. Struggle Model of Financial Change: Adaptation Results From Tension Between Vectors of Change and Vectors of Resistance.

regulated markets. The model treats political processes of *regulation* and economic processes of *regulatee avoidance* as opposing forces that, like riders on a seesaw, adapt continually to each other. This alternating adaptation is seen as a series of evolving lagged responses, with regulators and regulatees seeking to maximize their own objectives, conditional on how they perceive the opposing party to behave.

Two lags are featured: between regulation and avoidance (the *avoidance lag*) and between avoidance and re-regulation (the *re-regulation lag*). These lags result from various forms of resistance to change and differ systematically over time and across regulators, regulatees, and less-regulated players. It is hypothesized that the lags are, on average, longest for regulators (because of asymmetric information and because theirs is not a profit motivation) and shortest for self-selected less-regulated players.

To explain the proliferation of techniques for paying implicit interest and the evolution of substitutes for traditional deposit institutions and markets in the 1960s and 1970s, we need to incorporate into the regulatory dialectic the objectives of federal banking regulation and to identify outside forces that either accelerated or retarded the adjustment process. My analysis recognizes three disturbing exogenous forces: (1) state-of-the-art improvements in communications and computer technology; (2) the ratcheting upward movement of inflation and interest rates; and (3) increasing uncertainty about future movements in these variables. I hypothesize that, in the face of these environmental changes, the adaptive efficiency shown, on average, by less-regulated competitors exceeds that of deposit institution managers, and that the adaptive efficiency shown by these managers is greater than that shown by managers of competing state and federal banking agencies. Incorporating differential information, motivation, and adaptive capacity into the regulatory dialectic clarifies how increases in the pace of environmental change and in the degree of environmental uncertainty led profit-oriented responses from regulatees and less-regulated parties to come more quickly and regulatory responses to come more slowly. With the financial environment changing rapidly and becoming more uncertain, traditional strategies of monetary policy and deposit institution regulation were, for a time, overwhelmed by technological and policy-induced innovation.

Spreads Between Intermediary Borrowing and Lending Rates

Shape-shifting refers to transformations that are initiated by the transformee. Some authors [e.g., Niehans, 1978] look upon financial intermediation as a third-party process of transforming financial contracts. The conception is that financial intermediaries issue claims against themselves that differ from the securities they buy for their own account in one or more contractual features that the market implicitly or explicitly prices. Such features include: divisibility, redemption privileges, duration of the stream of promised payments, and default risk.

In combination with other macroeconomic forces, monetary and fiscal policies may be envisaged as impacting on short-term nominal rates of interest paid on default-free securities. Treating these rates as intermediaries' basic opportunity-cost rates for loanable funds, federal regulatory policies may be conceived as affecting—along with other microeconomic forces—different intermediaries' ability either to pay *temporarily* lower rates on various subsets of liabilities or to charge *temporarily* higher rates on various lending contracts.

I emphasize the word *temporarily* to recognize two important properties of a stationary capital-market equilibrium. Such an equilibrium would tend to develop whenever a fixed regulatory framework is held in place, irrespective of whether regulators designed that framework to benefit intermediaries, their funds suppliers, or their borrowing customers. First, in a stationary equilibrium, deposit institutions and other financial intermediaries must pay and charge the opportunity cost for loanable funds per se. Second, equilibrium spreads between financial intermediary borrowing and lending rates compensate institutions—again, at competitively determined prices—for the real costs of the transformation services they provide. For convenience in what follows, transformation costs are conceived as the sum of transactions costs and premiums for risk-bearing. By altering these costs, technological change and interest volatility impinge directly on the equilibrium value of intermediary spreads.

Forces Driving Contemporary Financial Change

In the real world, a stationary equilibrium is never precisely achieved because—as highlighted in the regulatory dialectic—exogenous and endogenous interventions occur in the equilibration process. Change is occurring so rapidly today that many financial institutions find it hard to distinguish their customers from their competitors. Moreover, their employees worry about hanging onto their jobs and fear that their expertise and job experience may possess little lasting market value. To put these fears and worries into focus, I want to identify the main forces driving financial change in the contemporary United States and examine adaptations to these forces that have proved especially successful.

Recent financial changes have been governed predominantly by three forces:

1. Technologial change
2. Volatility of inflation and interest rates
3. Preexisting patterns of financial regulation, which affect the adaptive efficiency of different institutions.

Technological Change

Technological advances are continually increasing the convenience of customer access to financial products and lowering the costs to institutions of providing that access. These changes may be described as the robotization and figurative electronic wiring of the system for delivering financial services to households and firms. We are not just replacing letters by electronic messages and thereby eliminating flows of paper evidences. We are taking people increasingly out of wholesale and (especially) retail financial processes. Their place is being taken by computer terminals activated by customer plastic cards or telephone calls and by online information files that are interchanged among institutions by cable or satellite communications links.

More than 100 regional electronic networks have been organized in the past three years and several national ATM networks are on the drawing boards. By year-end, as many as 60 U.S. banks will have an ongoing home-banking experiment incorporating videotechnology. Even bank robbers will be affected. To be maximally successful in the future, hold-up persons may have to learn to key their hold-up notes into a computer console.

Transactions terminals work faster and more accurately than the employees they displace. In an era of frequent redefinition of job activities, computer terminals are supremely adaptable. They can be taught a new task merely by connecting an accessory module or a new software package. They never unionize and don't insult shabby-looking customers. They are more reliable than human operatives in many ways. They are less dependable only in that terminal downtime shows a less predictable intraweekly pattern than human absenteeism and every data interchange exposes an institution to risks of hard-to-detect computer crime and invasions of privacy.

However, it would be a serious mistake to visualize the robotization of financial services as merely putting machines, such as ATMs, into roles formerly played by humans. A massive substitution of capital for labor simultaneously changes the essential nature of a firm's activities—the production processes it uses, the set of services it produces, and even its organizational structure.

The proximate impacts of robotizing and wiring financial-services delivery systems are: (1) to create scope economies which allow packages of complementary financial services to be produced more cheaply in combination than singly, and (2) to drive financial transactions costs steadily closer to zero. These changes in cost structure are narrowing deposit institution profit margins, extending the product lines of financial-services firms of all types, and making geographic distance between would-be transactors increasingly less-relevant factors in pricing financial services. In combination with the holding-company form of organization, electronic technology is converting what we used to call banking from a regional to an international industry and obliterating the distinction between bank and nonbank financial activities.

Volatility of Inflation and Interest Rates

Since 1965, interest rates have become so volatile that banks ought to experiment with flashing their current prime and CD rates in lights alongside their storefront time-and-temperature display. As macroeconomic policies have twisted and turned, interest rate volatility has transformed the maturity risk in the balance sheets of deposit institutions from a reliable source of average profit into a frequent source of substantial losses. For many S&Ls and mutual savings banks, interest-rate risk taken in the past threatens their institution's viability today. Hanging this sword over their heads has focused management attention on the very short run and led them to reposition their firms in ways that have progressively undercut their long-run share of the savings market. These institutions have survived into 1982 only because political pressure generated by the housing lobby let them lay off dangerous maturity risks ex post and ex ante onto their respective federal deposit insurance agency.

At the same time, interaction between fluctuating market interest rates and deposit-rate ceilings greatly influenced the speed and geographic spread of the robotization and electronic wiring of the system for delivering financial services to households and firms. The rate of diffusion of electronic-funds innovations depends very much on the level and pattern of expected future interest rates. This point is an important one. Even when explicit rates on commerical bank checking accounts were fixed at zero, deposit institutions were not always in a position to price electronic funds services favorably.

The ultimate payoff to an innovating intermediary is heavy in up-front costs and highly uncertain in any case. Start-up costs are substantial. What degree of penetration of competitors' markets and how high a volume of customer usage of cash-dispensing and teller machines are required to break even on electronic funds services depends on the ex ante opportunity cost of funds to the innovating institution. With financial services technology advancing rapidly, innovators also had to cover the risk of untimely obsolescence of physically adequate equipment. Finally, profitability calculations had to account for the possibility of untoward regulatory developments (e.g., mandatory sharing of equipment and successful locations on unfavorable terms). When it was not profitable to increase the rate of implicit interest, the robotization and electronic wiring of the financial system slowed noticeably. Whenever market interest rates moved below the ceiling rate on thrift institution passbook accounts, only managers preoccupied with long-run profits (an unusual breed indeed) showed much interest in ordering new electronic equipment.

Preexisting Financial Regulation and Differential Adaptive Efficiency

Changes in technology and in interest-rate volatility change the profitability and risks of financial intermediation. In the face of such developments, important differences in adaptive efficiency exist, as between regulated private firms, their less-regulated competitors, and government regulators. In an exogenously changing economy, government regulation acts, in part, as an inertial force. Regulation places an implicit tax on regulated firms. It reduces the adaptive capacity of regulated institutions by narrowing the set of economically feasible responses. Whether changes in the financial environment are favorable or unfavorable, managers of less-regulated competitors of deposit institutions can, on average, adapt to these changes more quickly and more efficiently than managers of regulated commercial banks and thrift institutions. In turn, deposit institution managers show, on average, greater adaptive efficiency in finding ways to circumvent traditional restrictions on their pricing, location, and business activities than managers of the several agencies that hold regulatory sway over deposit institutions show either in designing regulations or in closing loopholes which develop subsequently.

Operating at an informational disadvantage in a maelstrom of conflicting political pressures and governed by bureaucratic rather than profit incentives, regulatory agencies are typically slow to re-regulate. Regulatory paradigms change so slowly that one suspects that patterns of financial regulation prevailing in the future will prove a source of comfort to individuals who travel through time by the device of having their corpse frozen to await the development of a remedy for a currently incurable disease. Even if such individuals lie frozen for 50 years, regulatory lags make it possible that on revival they will find federal authorities still mispricing deposit insurance and still worrying about how to get S&Ls permanently back on their feet.

I believe that innovation becomes more intelligible if we posit three lags in the diffusion of financial innovations. I assume that these lags hold only on average, not for every individual innovation or for every entity involved.

1. The average lag in innovation by largely unregulated institutions behind state-of-the-art changes in technological and market opportunities
2. The average lag in innovation by regulated deposit institutions behind their less-regulated competitors
3. The average lag of regulatory responses behind innovations of both types.

The first lag reflects delays in project evaluation and gestation. We attribute the lag of regulated financial firms behind less-regulated ones to the self-selected aggressiveness of unconventional entrants into tightly regulated financial markets and to conscious and unconscious resistance to change by managements and employees at many of the established competitors. We trace the third lag to asymmetries in information, to the short horizons of political appointees, and to the characteristic slowness of bureaucratic decision making.

Innovation by Less-Regulated Institutions and Expansion of Deposit Institution Product Lines

The Money Market Fund

Growth in money market funds (MMFs) may be divided into three broad stages. Initial expansion in 1974–75 to $4 billion was supported by cost economies made possible by technological improvements in record-keeping and communications and driven by arbitrage opportunities opened up by government efforts to sustain a large gap between the low ceilings on yields that regulated deposit institutions could offer households on small-denomination short-term deposit instruments and the yields available to corporations and wealthy households on accumulations of $100,000 or more. Households of moderate means sought ways to pool smaller accumulations into $100,000 pieces. For such households, MMFs emerged as a particularly attractive pooling vehicle. Besides collecting and pooling funds from small savers, they also offered diversification and liquidity services. During 1976 and 1977, when market interest rates fell below deposit-rate ceilings on small-denomination deposits, MMFs sustained industry size at about $4 billion by increasing convenience yields by expanding customers' check and toll-free telephone redemption privileges.

In late 1977, as market yields rose above ceilings on small-denomination instruments, MMF growth began to surge again. During the 1978–82 period, deposit-institution regulators authorized their clients to issue a succession of new fund-raising instruments. These government-designed fund-raising options developed as a lagged regulatory response, aimed at reducing the exposure of regulated institutions to cherry-picking by MMFs.

Despite regulators' concerted efforts to be responsive to regulatee needs, during the last 5 years deposit institutions have found themselves regularly outcompeted by MMFs. The MMF industry now exceeds $220 billion in total assets. This growth has been built on the twin economic footing of operational efficiency and conservative positioning with respect to portfolio risk. Money market funds have exploited technological change to hold transaction costs down and have, on average, taken relatively little portfolio risk. Unlike the bulk of insured deposit institutions, they have marked their assets to market and closely controlled their exposure to maturity and default risk. Despite sharply increased volatility in market yields, MMFs' specialization in short-term assets has allowed them consistently to offer yields to small-denomination customers that closely track open-market yields on large-denomination instruments. This consistently good performance has demonstrated MMFs' ability to hedge both unanticipated inflation and disinflationary turns in monetary policy. MMFs' outstanding record is progressively lessening household fears about these funds' uninsured status. MMFs remain one of a precious few sets of financial institutions whose portfolio risks have not yet been assigned to a government insurance corporation.

Competitive and Regulatory Responses to Change in a Regulated Industry

Regulated Firms' Response to Technological Change. For an unregulated firm, an innovation can be justified only by demonstrating its technical productivity. To increase an unregulated firm's prospective profits, an invention must open up new markets or accomplish productive tasks better or more cheaply than preexisting arrangements. However, a preexisting burden of regulation produces rewards for doing things differently per se. Whether or not a particular innovation is technically advantageous, rearranging a deposit institution's formal organization (e.g., through affiliating with a holding company), its production processes, or its product lines promises to render obsolete particular elements and concepts of preexisting regulation. For this reason, in a regulated industry, managers have an incentive to track technological changes particularly closely and to contemplate their potential for developing loopholes in existing regulations. Technological change's potential for loophole productivity tends to temper innovation lags. It provides a counterbalance to institutional and regulator inertia and to management and employee resistance to change. At the same time, ongoing acts of innovation tend to lengthen and to exploit parallel regulatory lags that develop as regulators confront conceptual problems created by specific innovations and sort out political and economic pressures to decide what response (if any) to make to them.

Because robotization makes it cheaper to process customer transactions and to centralize the resulting records, it reduces the marginal cost to deposit institutions of offering additional customer services. By extending the range of an institution's feasible product mix, robotization simultaneously opens up vast possibilities for substituting away from regulated contracts and organizational forms and for making lightly burdened categories of time and savings accounts do the work of more heavily regulated transactions accounts.

Other things equal, robotization tends to favor larger and geographically more diversified firms. Every extension in the electronic system that links potential transactors figuratively by wire makes physical distance an increasingly less effective barrier to financial services competition.

These economic incentives for increased geographic and product diversification have led large deposit institutions to overcome regulatory barriers against such diversification by structurally locating various functional and regional activities in holding-company affiliates. This particular integrative strategy greatly multiplies the operative levels of supervisory authority, reinforcing the effects of robotization on the nature of financial services production. First, the need for executives in a holding-company structure raises the average skill level for surviving deposit institution employees. Second, a holding-company structure requires more complex patterns of internal information flow. For deposit institutions, this reinforces incentives for shifting accounting and pricing schemes away from discrete-time batch-processing technologies to continuous-flow real-time approaches.

Regulatory Response. Since interest rates surged again in late 1979, deposit institutions and their regulators have expressed a growing sense of crisis. Traditional approaches to deposit institution regulation have broken down under the twin pressures of unregulated competition and regulatee circumvention. Interest volatility and technological change have short-circuited preexisting structural controls on deposit institution activities, prices, and office locations. Although industry and regulatory shake-outs are well under way, the turmoil of conflicting interests has so far made a comprehensive regulatory solution politically infeasible.

Different views of what is an acceptable new regulatory pattern hold between banks and thrifts, between large and small depository firms, and between regulated and unregulated competitors. Crossfire from these institutions has kept Congress pinned on the sidelines, leaving competing regulators to protect their bureaucratic turf by fashioning piecemeal damage-control programs that tend to lag behind developments in the marketplace.

Until Congress decides to adjudicate the balance between new and old types of financial service providers, the regulatory paradigm for deposit institutions is one of grudging and partial relaxation of existing patterns of regulation. It shapes up as the regulatory equivalent of U.S. attempts to scale down its participation in the Vietnam War. Regulators' common goal is to find ways (such as the new money market account) to let their clientele deposit institutions extend their product lines and geographic reach and to unbundle the prices of the products and services they offer. This search is shifting the focus of deposit institution competition from implicit to explicit interest rates and explicit service fees, and from government-enforced regional and product-line cartels to self-selection of an appropriate range and quality of financial services.

Reputed Shifts in Money Demand

At the macroeconomic level, many observers view the proliferation of deposit substitutes and of schemes for paying implicit interest on demand and savings deposits as a series of unpredictable shifts in money demand (or in the velocity of money). While not technically wrong, this perspective is conceptually deficient in three ways.

First, what is unpredictable in the monetary-policy process is merely the timing and precise details of the particular innovations that occur. In the presence of ceilings on explicit rates of deposit interest, monetary restraint and other causes of cyclical and secular increases in market interest rates create clear and unsurprising incentives for institutions to innovate. These innovations take two forms: (1) finding ways to pay additional implicit interest, and (2) finding ways to substitute unregulated and less-regulated liabilities for sources of funding that are subject to aggregate control, deposit rate ceilings, reserve requirements, or deposit insurance assessments [Kane, 1979].

Second, although it is useful to distinguish the effect of innovations aimed at expanding implicit interest from the effect of innovations establishing new instruments, neither type of innovation must be presumed to affect the demand function for money. Rather than shifting the demand for money, innovations meant to increase implicit returns on customer accounts make explicit interest rates on these accounts a less-adequate index of the opportunity cost of money balances. The opportunity cost of money is the difference between the market yield on substitute assets and the explicit and implicit return on money itself. Once in place, schemes for expanding payments of implicit interest are relatively inflexible in a downward direction. At least in the short run, levels of implicit interest tend to remain high, even after market interest rates subsequently decline. This is particularly true of expansions in full-service branch offices or in off-premises teller machines. Since 1965, explicit returns on passbook funds, for example, have become an increasingly poor measure of the total (explicit and implicit) return on customer balances. Econometrically, the issue is less one of changes in the behavioral parameters of money demand than of drift in the mean and variance of errors in the interest-rate variable. At the same time, innovations that increase the availability of substitutes for traditional forms of money may be viewed as changing in an evolutionary manner the statistical definition of an invariant money concept. Certifiable changes in the set of monetary assets change aggregation procedures for calculating both the quantity of money and its own price, which is again an errors-in-variables problem. Of course, the problems introduced by the second type of innovation are more complex than those raised by the first type [Barnett, Offenbacher, and Spindt, 1981].

Third, advances in telecommunications and in information processing, that make assets such as money market mutual funds better substitutes for transactions balances simultaneously lower the marginal real cost of executing a round-trip investment in wholesale securities markets. This marginal cost should enter with a negative sign into any careful calculation of the relevant opportunity cost of securities investments. It is, in fact, a featured parameter in the inventory approach to money demand pioneered by Baumol (1952) and Tobin (1956). Secular declines in the implicit and explicit costs of brokerage services have made a progressively larger portion of quoted securities returns available as net yield to their owner.

In analyzing business investment, real after-tax and risk-adjusted interest rates are more relevant to investors than nominal yields on corporate securities. Similarly, in analyzing money demand, the differential between the rate of total return on a monetary aggregate and the net yield on securities is far more relevant than differences in explicit rates of return. Econometric studies that fail to model changing transactions costs and neglect the lagged cyclical variation and secular hysteresis in arrangements for paying implicit interest importantly misspecify the opportunity cost of money.

Future Patterns of Competition Between Deposit Institutions and Less-Regulated Intermediaries

Today, vultures are circling low over many deposit institutions. To shoo them away, deposit institutions of the future must become not only more like each other, but operate more like their less-regulated competitors: money market funds, brokerage houses, credit card companies, data-processing and communications firms, and large retailers, such as Sears. Adaptations to the traditional regulatory paradigm have left many deposit institutions with an inherited network of subsidized account-holder service departments and densely located full-service branch offices that cannot easily generate a sufficient flow of future fee and interest income to support themselves.

Deposit institutions' greatest need is to plug themselves squarely into the world of electronic finance. They must reconfigure their plant and equipment and their product mix to fit the emerging technological and competitive environments. They need to expand their electronic connections with potential customers (e.g., through home terminals and shared ATM networks) and with competitors of all kinds. ATM sharing is well under way among deposit institutions, and the securities industry has continued to show its adaptive efficiency by recognizing opportunities to service deposit institutions by acting as agents for their deposit customers.

In the 1980s, brokers have sought to sign up deposit institutions as wholesale clients. The first step took the form of designing futures-trading hedging-analysis programs for bank customers. In late 1981, several brokerage firms undertook to market All-Savers Certificates for participating deposit institutions. Beginning in June of 1982, Merrill Lynch set up a program in which it created a secondary market for 3.5-year negotiable CDs issued for marketing to Merrill account holders by participating deposit institutions. During the first six weeks of this program, Merrill marketed over $1 billion of these instruments for its deposit institution clients. Over the next two months, Dean Witter, Bache, and Shearson established similar programs.

By far the most dramatic industry crossovers have developed in connection with emerging asset-management packages designed by banks for their most affluent customers. Designed to compete head-to-head with brokerage cash-management accounts, these integrated accounts offer customers a combination of brokerage services, participation in a money market fund, checking, credit and debit cards, and a line of credit tied to securities held through the plan.

Discount brokers such as Quick & Reilly Inc., Charles Schwab & Co. Inc., and Fidelity Brokerage Services have been eager to collaborate with banks, who act as customer agents in ordering brokerage services. Similarly, banks and MMFs have developed the sweep account. In these accounts, a bank acts as the deposit institution customer's agent in collecting deposit balances in excess of a negotiated minimum and transmitting them to an MMF for investment in short-term market instruments. Both arrangements are completely legal, even though the Glass-Steagall Act prohibits deposit institutions from directly dealing in securities or offering a MMF.

Customer-sharing allows a bank to offer its customers brokerage services and bank-managed participation in the earnings of a MMF. Because these services expand discount brokers' and MMFs' preexisting role in the financial division of labor, deposit institution benefits from such connections are not merely those of circumventing federal restrictions on their investment-banking powers. After all, sweeping funds into a repo has long been standard for business customers. Even if banks and thrifts were free to operate brokerage departments or MMFs of their own, it is not clear that they could all do so efficiently or would (in any case) want to incur the development costs and long lead time required to develop an in-house program. Many of them (especially small community-oriented banks and most S&Ls) would be better off specializing in the activities they do best and contracting for these services from cost-efficient brokers and well-diversified MMFs, possessed of experienced managements and proven records. In asset-management arrangements, deposit institutions retain control of the client base and fee income. Still, linking brokerage and MMF accounts on line through banks can help brokers and MMFs, too. It familiarizes households with their names and improves the transferability of account funds. In particular, it can tie brokerage and MMF account balances directly into ATM and POS networks and catalogue-shopping schemes.

Sweep accounts are forms of networking in which firms share a single customer base. ATM networks are a form of facility sharing. These and other forms of sharing shape up as the major financial industry innovations of the 1980s. In the long run, many money market funds and brokerage firms may discover that their growth potential as electronically connected wholesale financial institutions dwarfs opportunities to operate as specialty shops for retail customers. Their best customers may prove to be financial institutions rather than households. In particular, MMF agency arrangements, such as sweep accounts, may prove even more useful to insurance companies and especially to pension funds.

Summary and Implications

Observed changes in the financial environment may be traced to impulses originating in one of three spheres of action:

1. the technological sphere:
   a. new production processes
   b. new products
   c. new sources of supply
2. the market sphere:
   a. shifts in customer demands
   b. competitor-initiated activity
      1) adaptations by existing competitors
      2) development of new entrants
3. the political sphere:
   a. societal attitudes
   b. laws and regulations
   c. penalties and enforcement.

Developments in any one sphere call for adaptive responses in the other spheres.

On the policy level, political developments may be envisaged as initiating changes in societal decisions about desirable microeconomic or macroeconomic time paths for income and its distribution. When sectoral political pressure on elected politicians to redistribute financial opportunities is effective, elected politicians usually establish a new agency or revise an existing agency's responsibilities. In turn, the affected regulatory agency ordinarily pursues its new responsibilities by setting up what it deems to be an appropriate framework for intervening in financial decisions. The regulatory rules and control procedures agency officials adopt necessarily alter the costs of staying or becoming competitive in the production and delivery of financial services. Such changes in cost structure establish incentives for regulated, less-regulated, and unregulated competitors to alter their product lines, organizational structure, and technology. This chain of adaptive response introduces unintended effects into the distribution of financial opportunities that generally prove contrary to the interest of the coalition that sponsored the focal regulations. These unintended effects tend to disrupt the commonality of interests and to weaken the political power of the sponsoring coalition. In the next round, only coalition members that remain unalienated can be counted on to lobby for re-regulation. Some groups in the original coalition will acquiesce in the unintended effects.

Monetary policy and policies aimed at regulating microeconomic competition among financial institutions work in many ways at cross-purposes. Adaptations by deposit institutions to monetary restraint tend to undermine the safety and soundness of the financial system and to deprive politically powerful sectors of the economy of financial opportunities. In turn, regulatory efforts to guarantee institutional soundness or to increase favored sectors' access to funds tend to undermine monetary control. In either case, the fundibility of financial products makes it hard to anticipate and to prevent circumvention of macroeconomic and microeconomic controls.

Psychologists tell us that business readjustments, changes in financial prospects, and expansion in one's product line or job activities are stressful enough to be health-threatening for managers forced to cope with them. This is as true for regulators as for regulatees. If salary scales for top bureaucrats continue to be squeezed by inflation and by state, local, and federal taxation, one has to wonder how agencies will recruit upper-echelon regulators whose experience, competence, integrity, and energy level can withstand the strain.

Note

1. Core Music Publishing, copyright 1981.

References

Barnett, William A., Edward K. Offenbacher, and Paul A. Spindt. "New Concepts of Aggregated Money." *Journal of Finance* 36 (May 1981), 497–505.

Baumol, William J. "The Transactions Demand for Cash: An Inventory Theoretic Approach." *Quarterly Journal of Economics* 66 (November 1952), 545–556.

Kane, Edward J. "Good Intentions and Unintended Evil: The Case Against Selective Credit Allocation." *Journal of Money, Credit and Banking* 9 (February 1977), 55–69.

Kane, Edward J. "The Three Faces of Commercial-Bank Liability Management." In *The Political Economy of Policymaking*, M. P. Dooley, H. M. Kaufman, and R. E. Lombra (Eds.). Beverly Hills: Sage Publication, 1979, pp. 149–174.

Kane, Edward, J. "Accelerating Inflation, Technological Innovation, and the Decreasing Effectiveness of Banking Regulation." *Journal of Finance* 36 (May 1981), 355–367.

Niehans, Jürg. *The Theory of Money*. Baltimore: Johns Hopkins University Press, 1978.

Tobin, James. "The Interest Elasticity of Transactions Demand for Cash." *Review of Economics and Statistics* 38 (August 1956), 241–247.

2 FINANCIAL INNOVATIONS AND FINANCIAL INSTABILITY: OBSERVATIONS AND THEORY

Hyman P. Minsky

Each year this conference seems to try to demonstrate its openness by having a "certified outsider" as a participant. The function of this certified outsider is to present an alternative view that unwittingly will reinforce the strength of belief of the true believers in the validity of maintained monetarist doctrine. This year I expect that I am this beast. No matter what the overt subject of my talk may be, its covert function, in the minds of the organizers, is to reinforce belief in monetarist precepts, presumably by revealing the emptiness of at least one of the alternatives.

I accepted the invitation to participate because this conference is on my home ground and, in this era of austerity, I saved the government the expense part of the price of a participant. Furthermore, although I don't expect I'll be able to penetrate the tight beliefs of the true believers, I hope that there are some here who will pay attention to the substance of my remarks, which no matter what the overt subject, is a statement of the *financial instability hypothesis*. This view has often been phrased as an interpretation of Keynes, but it has older and perhaps even deeper roots in economic theory than Keynes.[1]

Incidentally, as a certified outsider, I enjoy being at a meeting of "true believers". When I meet with allies and associates, I sometimes begin to suspect the validity of my special views; when I meet with either monetarists or orthodox Keynesians, I find my belief in my deviant views reinforced by the strange beliefs of orthodox economists. By being here these two days, I expect that my degree of rational confidence in the validity of the financial instability hypothesis will increase.

I expect that many monetarists must feel the way I do, in that they would much rather stand on their own views without having to defend or rest their case upon the views of others, no matter how much of an intellectual debt they may owe to the others. In a similar fashion, I wish to draw away from claiming to interpret Keynes correctly, i.e., that my view is the true interpretation of a sacred text, and rest the case for the set of constructs and ideas I put forth on their relevance to our type of economy. Although much of what I say is based on an interpretation of Keynes' *The General Theory* that I put forth some years ago,[2] my thinking has developed in a number of ways in the years since I wrote that little book.[3] In particular, the integration of investment and the deficit and the commitments embodied in liability structures, which rests upon Kalecki and Keynes in rather equal measure, was missing from my work of a decade or so ago.[4] Although I feel I owe a great deal to Keynes, my debts go beyond Keynes. I would not want my economics of 1982 to be judged on whether it is true to Keynes. Incidentally, I owe a substantial intellectual debt to Henry Simons, a Chicago economist who was a contemporary of Keynes ["Rules vs. Authorities" and *The General Theory* are both of 1936].[5]

Bluntly put, the financial instability hypothesis holds that the normal functioning of our type of economic order—i.e., a capital-using capitalist economy with a financial system that is complex, convoluted, and evolving—leads to business cycles and, from time to time, these cycles include threats of the incoherence of a runaway inflation or a debt deflation and deep depression. In particular, what happened fifty years ago (1932–33) was not, and must never be, considered as a freak event or an event that was caused by incompetence or malevolence. It was neither the malefactors of great wealth, the ineffectiveness of Mr. Hoover, the abdication of responsibility by the Federal Reserve, nor the various efforts by the Congress to stem the tide that caused the Great Collapse. The cause was in the nature of our type of market economy. Policy intervention and the particulars of the institutional structure affect the details but not the essentials of the processes that lead to instability.

Even though the start of the economy on a route that leads to 1929–33 seems to be a normal result of market processes, policy and the institutional structure affect what happens. The result of the processes need not be a great depression. Policy interventions of a lender of last resort nature and the impact of big government and the deficits it generates when income falls have succeeded in containing the thrust towards deep depressions. However, the medicine that succeeded—like most powerful medicine—has side effects. The inflation, stagflation, and turbulence since 1966 are prices paid, in our times, for not having deep depressions.

My interpretation of the political success of Reaganomics, which promised a free-lunch move toward permanent bliss, is that, in the minds of the electorate, the side effects of the measures that have been successful in containing the downside thrust of the economy in the years since the mid-1960s outweigh the benefits of not having had a major depression. The electorate does not appreciate the depth of what happened fifty years ago and, I venture to assert, neither does a majority of the discipline. As a result, neither the electorate nor the discipline appreciates how great a success we have enjoyed in not having a depression in the 37 years since World War II.

The electorate and the discipline are well aware of inflation and a sluggish economy. This awareness of shortcomings and disregard of success is a triumph of propaganda and restricted vision over knowledge of history. The blinders placed on economists by the neoclassical synthesis effectively filters observations of the economy. In neoclassical theory, by the late 1960s the Great Depression became a nonevent. The Reagan program, if fully effected, will result in the reconstruction of an economy in which a great depression is possible. However, the greed unleashed in 1981, as the revenue system was compromised, has put the economy into a fiscal posture with a structural inflationary bias and a monetary posture that attempts to offset this bias by repressing investment and resource creation. Whether this combination will so distort the financial structure and so inhibit the Federal Reserve from acting as an effective lender of last resort that a great contraction results, only time will tell. The impossible, another great collapse, can become possible if structural changes now on the agenda are effected.

Significance of the Great Collapse

It is a common assertion that one picture is worth a thousand words. Similarly, one counterexample is worth a thousand theorems that claim universality. Standard economic theory aims to explain how the decentralized market mechanism, in which trading is guided solely by self-interest, leads to a coherent outcome; i.e., a system that on the surface seems to be conducive to the emergence of chaos has a deep structure that leads to coherence. One counterexample to the claim of universality for the coherence theorems is the Great Collapse of 1929–33. The interaction among markets that led to the Great Collapse was described beautifully by I. Fisher in various places.[6] Before this collapse was ended by intervention in March of 1933, the state of the economy could aptly be defined as chaotic. What is there about an economy so that its normal functioning leads to an evolution from the tranquil progress of 1946–66 to turbulence and periodic threats of collapse?

An economy with capital assets, investment, and our type of financial structures can be characterized as an interactive system in which outcomes of today become inputs of tomorrow. Whereas simple linear interactive systems are mathematically tractable (I know, for I exploited this tractability in a series of articles),[7] until the advent of a serious capacity to simulate with the age of computers, the time paths generated by nonlinear dated interactive systems could not be traced. It is now well known that, as a general rule, complex time interdependent nonlinear systems lead to exotic time series in which initially coherent behavior breaks down into turbulence (or incoherence), which then may be succeeded by another period of apparent turbulence. Furthermore, the evidence from simulations indicates that it is reasonable to conjecture that chaotically unstable trajectories are more likely to occur with less nonlinearity for multiequation models.[8]

R. Day experimented with a number of models that led to chaotically unstable trajectories and reported his results in the June 1982 *AER*. In each run reported, the model generated apparently coherent time series for a while, only to have unstable trajectories emerge. We can distinguish between the free fall of a time-dependent process, in which the past of the system fully determines today's variables, and constrained behavior, in which some of the system-determined variables are not allowed to rule but are replaced by exogenously determined variables (ceilings, floors, institutional rigidities, policy interventions, etc.). These dominating exogenous variables, together with the allowed endogenous variables, are the initial conditions for future runs of the system. Thus, the apt model for studying our economy, which is a complex iterative system with nonlinearities due to accumulations of capital and debts, implies that chaos is an endogenously generated result; but the system may be constrained from achieving chaos by apt interventions that break into the progression to chaos.

For quite a time now, Frank Hahn, perhaps because he is the neoclassical theorist in Cambridge, has been insisting that there is no ground in the Arrow-Debreu results for assuming a moving Walrasian Equilibrium as the natural state of a capitalist economy with money.[9] That is, once money and capital assets are introduced in any serious way, the theorems of Arrow-Debreu do not carry through. Thus the basic monetarist set-up, which assumes the existence of a moving equilibrium which is disturbed by monetary changes, is not a valid game; the equilibrium which was assumed to exist in truth does not exist. The mathematical results that Day reports indicate that the normal workings of our economy lead to periods of robust expansion, almost regardless of policy intervention, that are followed by chaos, unless apt interventions take place.

It is nice to have mathematical models of economic interactions to point to as validating the general position that the normal processes of our economy imply the emergence of chaos, i.e., the market mechanism breaks down. The existence of such formal models carries little weight unless processes in and observations of our economy indicate that progressions toward an unstable regime do take place. The evidence for the thrusts to financial instability, aside from the fact that it occurred in history, lies in the changing relation between debts and incomes, the variable margins of safety in financing contracts, and the evolution of financial practices over time.

The Great Collapse is the counterexample to the universality of the assertion that decentralized markets lead to coherence. We know that multiequation iterative processes that are not linear generate time series that exhibit chaos. The Great Collapse of 1929–33 is an example of chaotic behavior. We now have to link chaotic behavior to observable developments in the economy.

Financial Innovations

> That the effort by the central bank to control inflation abets the development of unstable conditions in the money market may seem to be a dismal conclusion. Actually, it is too much to expect that a trivial set of operations such as those labeled monetary policy or fiscal policy will always succeed in maintaining stability in a dynamic economy. Institutional innovation is one aspect of a dynamic economy and money-market innovations occur in response to the needs of a growing economy. That these changes will tend to undermine the effectiveness of stabilization policies is a by-product of growth.
>
> However, the role of the central bank is not really diminished by the recognition of its ineffectiveness in preventing inflation as well as in stemming deflation. The central bank's function is to act as a lender of last resort and therefore to limit the losses due to the financial crisis which follows from the instability induced by the innovations during the boom. A combination of rapid central bank action to stabilize financial markets and rapid fiscal policy action to increase community liquidity will minimize the repercussions of the crisis upon consumption and investment expenditures. Thus a deep depression can be avoided. The function of central banks therefore is not to stabilize the economy so much as to act as a lender of last resort. This they are able to do.[10]

> "Repercussions from Penn Square's collapse are spreading to smaller banks and exploration concerns, as lenders alter criteria for making energy-industry loans and emphasize borrowers' cash flow."[11]

The above quotations, one from the conclusion of my "Central Banking and Money Market Changes" of 1957 and the other from the *Wall Street Journal* (July, 1982) summarize my views about the significance of financial innovations. It is now twenty-five years since I concluded that "the function of central banks therefore is not to stabilize the economy but to act as a lender of last resort." At the time I wrote "Central Banking and Money Market Changes," instability of the kind we had had prior to World War II and since the middle 1960s was not a clear and present danger. The credit crunch of 1966, which brought forth Federal Reserve lender of last resort intervention in order to contain a threatened debt deflation, was almost a decade in the future. Nevertheless, the portfolio adventuring that led to the current fragile structure was taking place in the 1950s; the trend toward, if not the achievement of, financial fragility (which is a necessary but not sufficient condition for instability) was evident in the innovations in financial markets that were taking place.

The specific money market innovation that prompted the writing of "Central Banking and Money Market Changes" was the emergence of the modern Federal Funds Market. I happened to spend some weeks in 1955 observing operations on Wall Street. I was fortunate to catch the Federal Funds Market at an early stage. I recall the mimeographed worksheets at Garvin-Bantel and the eccentric pattern of the banks that dealt in Federal Funds. The Federal Funds Market is significant in that it enables a given volume of reserves to carry a larger volume of bank liabilities and thus earning assets, and that it changes the way banks make position.

The development of the Federal Funds Market marked a shift by banks from making position by Treasury debt to making position by buying money through a set of devices, such as Federal Funds, Certificates of Deposits, Commercial Paper, Eurodollar borrowings, and varieties of repurchase agreements. The growth of the Federal Funds Market—like all market developments—was a response to profit-making opportunities. This change increased the volume of financing that was available with a given reserve base. The ability to increase available financing in response to profit opportunities by way of institutional innovations indicates that, in our type of economy, the supply of finance that is available through banks and other financial institutions responds to the demand for finance. As I argue in "Central Banking and Money Market Changes" and in other places, this responsiveness of supply to demand imposes a potential upward instability to the system. Steady noninflationary expansion can give way to an accelerating inflationary expansion once the supply of finance is responsive to demand. With an endogenous supply of finances, stable expansion destabilizes the economy; stable expansion is impossible.

When we think of instability, in particular in the context of the lender of last resort responsibilities of the Federal Reserve, our concern is with downward instability. However, before the threat of downward instability can be serious, the liability structure has to be complex, so that a systemic failure to validate a set of liability structures because profits fall or other costs rise will lead to an attempt to unwind liability structures. Attempts to unwind have serious implications for asset prices, financing possibilities, and, therefore, investment. Before downward instability is a threat, it is necessary to have a period of financial innovation during which the complexity of liability structures increase. These prior developments imply an upward instability to the economy.

Positions in capital assets and financial instruments are financed by liabilities, which in a closed economy are owned by households, either directly or through a layer of institutions. Any innovation in finance that increases the availability of finance for the holding of capital assets or financial instruments tends to increase either the quantity held or the price per unit. Given that in the short run the stock of capital assets is fixed, this implies that financial innovations tend to raise the prices of elements in the stock of capital assets: Higher capital asset prices, for an unchanged expected stream of profits, implies a lower implicit interest rate on real assets.

Positions in capital assets in "embryo" (i.e., investment outputs) need to be financed. Financial innovations increase the availability and lower the cost of financing for investment. [One spectacular innovation of the past 20 years was the use of REITs to finance construction.] For investment projects with significant gestation periods, interest costs on early inputs can be a large part of the supply price, once interest rates are at interesting levels.

Financial innovations increase the supply of finance for positions in capital assets, which raises capital asset prices, even as they increase the supply of finance for investment, thus lowering the supply price of investment output. The gap between capital asset prices and investment output prices, in the context of given criteria for financing investment, is a determinant of investment: The greater the gap, the greater the level of investment. Furthermore, for given criteria for financing investment, the greater the gap, the higher the incremental leverage ratio. Financial innovations, which are a response to profit opportunities, lead to an increase in aggregate profits because they facilitate increased investment which leads to higher profits. A self-reinforcing process exists in a modern capitalist economy in the connections among financial innovations, the financing of investment, and realized profits.

However, even as financial innovations increase investment and profits now, they increase the sensitivity of the system to rising interest rates. Financial innovations are a response to rising interest rates. These innovations effectively increase the income foregone by holding liquid assets. During the time a financial innovation is working its way through the economy, interest rates tend to be lower than they would have been in the absence of the innovation. As an innovation matures, the supply curve of finance might be infinitely elastic at a plateau but, as the innovation works its way through the economy, the downside effect of innovation is attenuated. When this happens, interest rates rise. This leads to a rise in the cash flow required to validate the debts that reflect the increased leverage made possible by the innovation. As a result, the profits and expected profits share of gross capital income will decline. This will lead to a slowdown of investment and, therefore, of gross capital income.

Financial innovation increases the financing available with a given reserve base and the momentum of an investment boom draws forth creative financing as interest rates increase. Financial innovation enables expansion to lead to inflation. The impact on interest rates of inflation and of the attempts by the monetary authorities to slow inflation, leads to further sharp increases in interest rates. It is clear from 1966, 1969, 1974, and 1981–82 that the high and rising interest rate inflationary mode of operation of the economy will continue until a break in the financial system—a credit crunch—occurs. A credit crunch alters criteria for making loans. But such a change means a sharp fall in some asset values and a decline in profits. The protections given to debt owners by cash flows and market values decreases, lowering the value of debt. The change from an inflationary expansion with momentum that has convoluted the financial structure involves serious risks of a financial debacle: the events of 1982 bear this proposition out.

The Theory of Economic Instability

To link profit-seeking behavior in financial markets and endogenously generated economic instability requires an economic theory in which instability is a normal functioning event. To understand what this requires, it is necessary to get down to the fundamentals of economic theory; in particular, to delimit what can and what cannot be asserted as valid on the basis of economic theory. What is the primary question that economic theory must address? This basic question is rarely addressed in today's high technology discipline. However, we must speak to this question because the meaning and significance of financial innovation, of monetarism, and of the various attempts to understand Keynes all rest on the answer to this question.

There are really two branches of economic theory, and they have little in common. In the American discipline, one branch is only minimally represented, whereas in Europe and Britain, the balance is more even. Even so, the distinction between the two branches is hardly ever clearly made. Both branches are to be found in the work of Smith. Smith really posed two questions for theory. These were:

1. Why do decentralized markets, which on the surface should lead to chaos, lead to coherent outcomes? (This is the invisible hand.)[12]
2. Why is one country richer or poorer than another? or, alternatively, What determines the progress or degradation of an economy through time?

Standard American economic theory addresses the first question. The Arrow-Debreu model may well be taken as an end result of the analysis of Smith's first question. The quantity theory of money is grafted onto the Arrow-Debreu model in an effort to address the second question. However, the logical flaws in the treatment of capital assets in the neoclassical growth models that were revealed in the two-Cambridge Debate show that the basic belief of the monetarist school—that there exists an equilibrium growth rate determined by the Walrasian model—is false.[13] There is no way to transform the demonstration that an equilibrium exists in trading markets and/or in models of production with given resources into a model of the accumulation of capital. In particular, no theorems of the existence, stability, and optimum characteristics of a decentralized market system in which accumulation and finance exist have been demonstrated.

In order to handle accumulation, economic theory has to conceive of the economy as an iterative process in which limits to today's behavior are determined by the accumulated results of past performance and today's behavior reflects views as to the future performance of the economy. The second school of economics starts with the problem of accumulation in a capitalist economy. The object is to explain differential richness and the course of richness and resource utilization over time. How to explain investment—or resource creation—is the question, and, in particular, the problem is specified to be the analysis of resource accumulation under capitalist conditions.[14]

One way of distinguishing between the two views of theory is to examine the parable with which a heuristic exposition of each theory begins. The parable for resource utilization theory is that of traders at a village fair, where each actor has an initial bundle of goods, such that mutually beneficial trading can occur. The parable for the accumulation theory is that of a conference between bankers and businessmen in a board room where the subject is the financing of activity. Another way of distinguishing between the two types of theory is that one—the theory that derives coherence from a set-up that seemingly would have chaos as its normal outcome—claims to be general, independent of institutional specifics; whereas the theorems of the accumulation paradigm theory depend upon institutional detail. The economy behaves differently with a big government and intervention than with a small government and laissez-faire in the accumulation but not in the resource use theory.

It is obvious that the line of theorizing that followed Keynes and the classics missed the point because it largely ignored the distinction between the economics of resources creation—which is where Keynes sits—and the economics of resource utilization, which is the problem that is central to the classical school.[15] The formulation of the difference between theories that has been put forth here was not really available until after the two-Cambridge Debate clarified the tautology in the orthodox treatment of capital and the precise statement of the content of price theory by Arrow-Debreu made the limited domain of relevance of general equilibrium theory clear.

The real victim of the two-Cambridge Debate and the Arrow-Debreu theory is the neoclassical synthesis. There is no way of integrating Keynes and the classics, once Keynes is interpreted as a statement of an accumulation-oriented theory that fully allows for the institutional detail of the financing of asset accumulation and holding. To understand the accumulation view of a capitalist economy, it is necessary to explore the implications of an uncompromising Wall Street view of our economy.

The Wall Street View

Let us take an unambiguous and uncompromising Wall Street view of our type of economy. The subject of this view is the financing of activity, which really has two aspects:

1. the financing of the use of existing resources
2. the financing of positions in the stock of capital assets.

Part of the use of existing resources is to produce additions to the stock of capital assets, i.e., investment. Thus the financing of investment is covered by the first heading.

The question that always arises in Wall Street is: What is the apt liability structure for financing holdings of particular sets of capital assets that are used for the production and distribution of the commodities that trading games economics deal with? Obviously, this question of the apt liability structure for financing various types of activity is what Penn-Square, Penn-Central, International Harvester, Chrysler, and the Dupont acquisition of Conoco deal with. It also was what the life, times, and business activity of J. P. Morgan were about. It is, in short, what banking, generically defined, is about.[16]

Three aspects of the banking business are critical to the Wall Street perspective:

1. the financing of positions in capital assets
2. the financing of investment
3. the financing of the bank's position.

The first two deal with the asset side of banks or the assets bank's broker. The liability side of banking arises because there are banks that take positions in assets that need to be financed. Therefore, in the background of discussion about financing investment or financing positions in capital assets in the Wall Street view, is a question of the liability structures by which banking institutions finance their activities. In a banking structure, one outcome of the financing of position and investment can be the issuance of negotiable and demand liabilities; negotiable demand liabilities of banks are money.

Money, therefore, is a product of financing activity; it is endogenous to the economy. When a unit holds money, it has title to a liability on a bank's balance sheet; this liability, together with other liabilities, finance the bank's position. Inasmuch as the banking institution has such demand liabilities, a major activity of a bank is the financing and refinancing of its position. In the language that follows, banks are speculative or rollover financing institutions.[17]

Let us return to a fundamental question of monetary theory: What is the apt liability structure for financing a position in capital assets? This is a problem in corporate finance. The basic credit evaluation by bankers consists of estimating cash flows; credit is available exactly as the cash flows envisaged in the credit analysis are more than sufficient by some margin to meet the payment commitments on the debts. Collateral is of secondary importance as compared to cash flows from operations. Collateral can be interpreted as a potential generator of cash flows if the prospective profits that are the normal determinant of the willingness to finance are not forthcoming. The market value of collateral is the capitalized value of future cash flows.

The contracts out of which money arises involve commitments to make payments of money to a bank. In a banking system, money is regularly destroyed as the payment commitments on such contracts are fulfilled. In a well-functioning banking system, the amount paid to the banks by borrowers exceeds by a margin (the interest on the loan) the amount paid by the banks to or for the borrower. This reflux, which destroys money, was, in some older doctrines, supposed to protect against excessive creation of credit. (The validity of the reflux view is not the issue here.) The issue is that well-structured bank loans lead to money creation now and money destruction later. Presumably, the credit analysis that led to the bank financing of projects determined that the cash flow to the businesses—the prospective profits of businesses—were sufficient to assure that payments would be made. But if the payment commitment on debts lead to a destruction of bank money, then the later debtors will find money scarce. The borrowing and repaying game of financing will work only if bank financing maintains and even increases outstanding bank liabilities in the interval between the loan and the repayment.

There is a two-way process by which bank financing increases the level of total demand even as the repayment of debt to banks both decreases the money supply and leads to income escaping from the circuit of demand. These leakages of income must be offset. This requires that a sufficient quota of loans deemed to be well-structured are approved by bank lending officers over each time interval.

A banking system finance approach to money makes money one output of the ruling financing arrangements. The question is what determines the demand and the supply for financing. In a world with complex financing structures where the basic financing act is an agreement to finance and where liabilities can become generally acceptable by endorsement, the amount of money is endogenous; the supply of money adjusts to the demand for financing.

A strong demand for the financing of investment relative to the supply from existing channels and institutions will lead to the development of new institutions and new usages. Excess or growing demand for financing implies profit opportunities in financing—which, in turn, implies that entrepreneurial initiative will take advantage of the differentials among available terms that develop.

In a financing structure, payment commitments on account of principal and interest on liabilities are related to cash flows from operations in one of three ways:

1. cash flows sufficient to meet all payment commitments
2. cash flows sufficient to meet interest payments on liabilities but not repayment of principal
3. cash flows not sufficient to meet all of interest, let alone principal. I have labeled these hedge, speculative, and Ponzi finance. Over an era of successful functioning of the economy, the proportion of speculative (i.e., rollover) financing to hedge financing increases. This is an empirical development that takes place because, over a period of successful functioning, business is able to rollover maturing debt. The supply of short-term funds is increased due to financial innovations because, in the main, financial innovations are ways of exploiting and putting to use prior pools of liquid assets.[18]

In an economy, the sum of deficits over all sectors must sum to zero. The profit share of income, under strong assumptions, equals investment plus the government deficit. In this essential equality, profits are the gross capital income. The liability structure determines how profits are distributed between debtors, equity holders, and retained earnings of businesses (all gross). When financial innovation as well as the creation of financing through normal banking structures leads to investment expansion then profits increase, if there is no offset through the government budget or foreign trade. In a closed capitalist economy with no government, aggregate profits equal investment; in a closed capitalist economy with large government, aggregate profits equals investment plus the deficit. If the government deficit is inversely related to employment levels, then a strong debt deflation cannot take place if government is big, because the cash flows to pay debts cannot fall as far and as fast in response to an investment decline as they would if government is small.[19]

The view of gross capital income as the sum of investment plus the deficit—under special assumptions about savings out of profits and out of wage incomes—and the schema of hedge, speculative, and Ponzi finance combine to give us an endogenous generation of instability in our economy. The cash payment commitment on liabilities that make a unit a hedge, speculative, or Ponzi finance unit are functions of the interest rate. Inasmuch as speculative units are such because they finance part of their position on short term, a rise in interest rates will transform hedge units into speculative units, speculative units into Ponzi units, and Ponzi units, which in effect capitalize interest, into units whose expected cash flows, when capitalized out to whatever horizon may be chosen, are unlikely to fulfill all commitments on debts. That is, with given gross capital incomes, Ponzi units become bankrupt when interest rates become high and stay high.

Investment takes place because the present value of gross capital income expected from utilizing investment goods as capital assets exceeds the supply price of investment output by a good enough margin so that financing for investment activity and the subsequent holding of the capital assets is available. But rising interest rates decrease the value of capital assets, even as they increase the supply price of investment output. Thus, rising interest rates will decrease investment unless the realized and expected cash flows from operations (for example, gross capital income) increases. A cumulative process in which rising profits more than offset the increase in interest rate occurs when financial innovations suppress the rise in the rate of interest. However, as demand for financing builds up and as the Federal Reserve in response to inflation dampens the rate of expansion through banks, rising interest rates will dominate the current realized and the expected improvement in profits. This will decrease investment.

High interest rates and the decline in gross capital income lead to further unplanned and undesired shifts from hedge to speculative to Ponzi finance. The result will be a cumulative debt deflation, unless the fall in gross capital income is offset by either sharp declines in interest rates or developments that sustain gross capital income.

In our experience since the midsixties, sharp declines in interest rates followed lender of last resort interventions even as large government deficits sustained gross capital income. Instability has been contained because government deficits have sustained gross capital incomes.

Lender of Last Resort Interventions

Figures 2–1 and 2–2, which are borrowed from Professor E. I. Altman's June 1982 statement to a House subcommittee, give us a balance sheet and income flow perspective on the changes in the way business finances positions in assets and the cash flow commitments embodied in liability structure.[20] Parallel with these developments, there was a rise in the banking and financial systems' loans/asset ratio and the proportion of bought money in total bank liabilities.

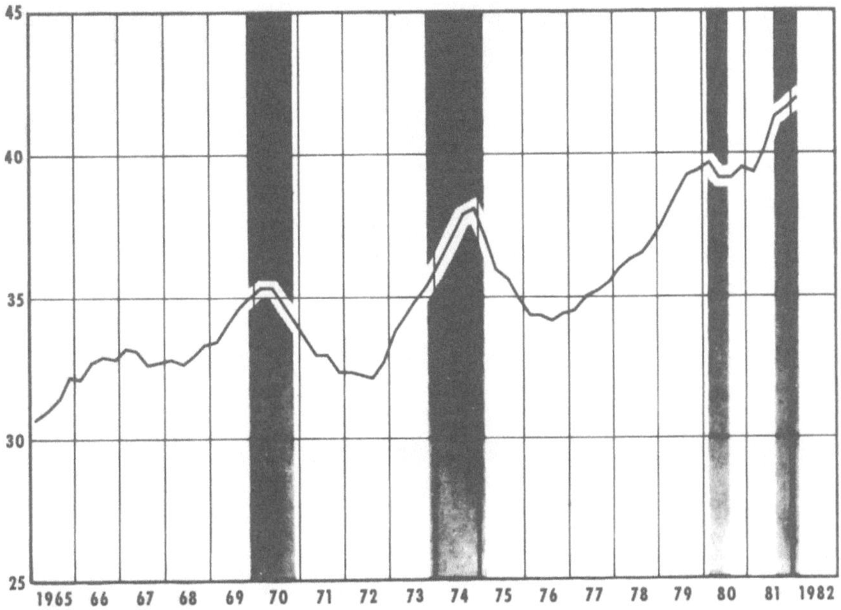

Figure 2-1. Short-term Debt as a Percent of Total Debt, Nonfinancial Corporations. Flow of Funds, Quarterly Data at Seasonally Adjusted Annual Rates. Data for 1982-Q1 are Preliminary. *Note*: Shaded areas denote recessions as defined by NBER. [Taken from: Prof. E. I. Altman (NYU) Statement, June 23, 1982. Subcommittee on General Oversight, Committee on Small Business, House of Representatives].

In the 1960s, about a third of business debt was short term; in the 1980s, this ratio is about 40 percent. This is not a dramatic increase, but as is well known, debt became a higher percentage of total liabilities over this period. By 1965, the beginning of Altman's figure, short-term debt was a significantly larger proportion of total liabilities of firms than earlier in the postwar period.

The second figure tells a more dramatic story. It chronicles a startling rise in net interest payments as a percent of capital income [the sum of gross profits before taxes, interest paid (net), and rent] from approximately 8 percent in 1965 to about 42 percent in early 1982. The figure can be viewed as tracing the mean of a frequency distribution. It is obvious that the likelihood of a substantial number of firms having to pay more in interest than

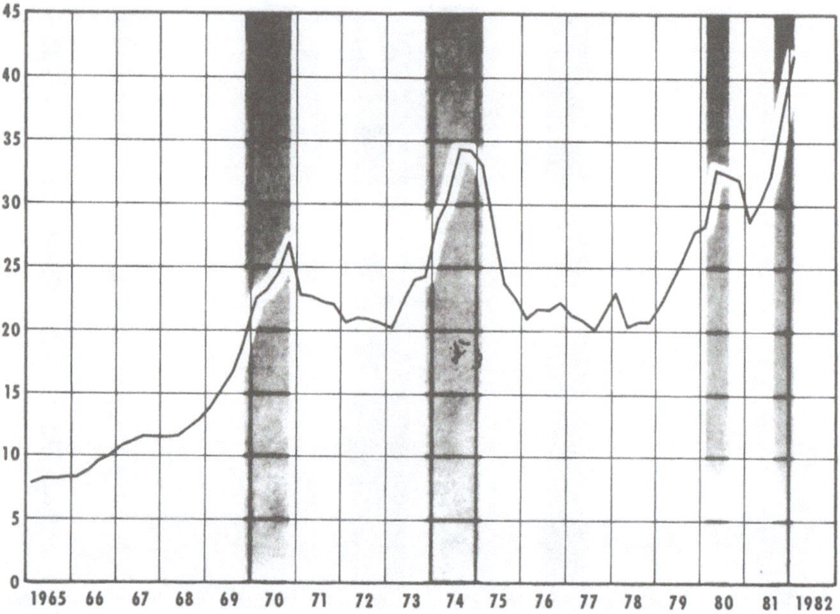

Figure 2-2. Net Interest Payments as a Percent of Capital Income, Nonfinancial Corporations. Capital Income is Economic Profits Before Tax Plus Net Interest Payments. Department of Commerce, National Income and Product Accounts. Quarterly data at seasonally adjusted annual rates. Data for 1982-Q1 are preliminary and based on estimates of net interest payments by the Federal Reserve Board staff. *Note*: Shaded areas denote recessions as defined by NBER. [Taken from Prof. E. I. Altman (NYU) statement June 23, 1982. Subcommittee on General Oversight, Committee on Small Business, House of Representatives].

available funds from operations was much greater in 1982 than in 1966.

The trend and the cycle in the ratio of net interest payments to capital income that is sketched in figure 2–2 is compounded out of three parts:

1. the debt component in the liability structure
2. the behavior of interest rates
3. the path of the denominator-gross capital income.

The cyclical peaks in this ratio come in recessions and quite apparently reflect the effect of shortfalls in capital income and peaks in interest rates.

If we integrate the developments shown in the figures with our knowledge of recent cycle experience, the sharp falls in the ratio of short-term to total debt that began during the recessions of 1970 and 1974 are associated with a funding of short-term debt into long-term debt as interest rates fell. The decline in the net interest payments as a percent of capital income reflects the fall in interest rates and a rise in capital income as an expansion matures. In both 1970 and 1974, improvements in these ratios took place after the crunch. The Penn-Central crisis (with Chrysler finance involvement) in 1970 and the Franklin National/REIT debacle in 1974–75 are the identifying labels for these episodes. In each case, the crunch brought forth lender of last resort interventions by the Federal Reserve system.

The Federal Reserve is organized as a bank. It can affect markets by investing, lending, or endorsing (extending protection to or blessing). The Federal Reserve wears two hats: it is part of the government apparatus that attempts to put overall income, employment, and prices on track; and it is the key organization that is responsible for the normal functioning of the financial system. This responsibility for normal functioning has two aspects: (1) to assure that financing is available for well-structured projects at terms that are consistent with the prospective cash flows; and (2) to abort any iterative debt deflation process that may be triggered. But the only way the Federal Reserve can assure the availability of financing or abort a debt deflation process is by either investing or lending; i.e., by increasing its liabilities, which are currency and bank reserves.

The Federal Reserve allowed its behavior with respect to its mission to cooperate in trying to keep the economy on path to be determined by monetarist precepts and to dominate its responsibility to assure that financing is available at terms that are consistent with cash flows during the inflationary expansions that led up to the recessions of 1969–70, 1974–75 and 1979 to date. But such Federal Reserve behavior implies that interest rates rise to extreme heights, so that the ratio of interest payments to capital income rises. A rise in interest rates leads to a breakdown in long-term debt markets. As a result, both interest rates and the ratio of short-term debt in total debt increases. These changes will transform hedge financing units into speculative financing units and speculative financing units to Ponzi units. With sufficient capitalizing of interest, the equity protection to lenders disappears. As this happens to a bank, a savings intermediary, or a business organization, maturing short-term liabilities cannot be rolled over.

At this stage, for banks and thrift institutions, the FDIC, the FSLIC, or the Federal Reserve steps in and refinances the threatened organizations. Using discretion, which reflects its evaluation of the seriousness of the situation, the Federal Reserve will move to facilitate the refinancing of exposed positions by either lending to exposed institutions or by buying securities on the open market. When the Federal Reserve does this, it drops its presumed responsibility for constraining or inducing monetary growth (whatever that may be). At this stage the Federal Reserve has only two interests:

1. to assure that refinancing is available to markets that are threatened
2. to set financing terms at levels that will reverse the shift towards the Ponzi end of the financing spectrum.

But the only ways the Federal Reserve can achieve such objectives is by acquiring assets or extending guarantees that, if necessary, it will acquire assets. But if the Federal Reserve needs to acquire assets either by open market operations or through the discount window (omitting the extension of guarantees technique which really only postpones the need to increase reserves), the Federal Reserve has given up control over the reserve base. Even if we ignore the impact of international finance and the currency ratio, the Federal Reserve, over the period in which it is acting as lender of last resort, has no effective control over the volume of its own liabilities it creates.

In the era since 1966, Federal Reserve interventions as a lender of last resort, combined with the effect of government deficits in sustaining cash flows to business, have succeeded in containing the impact of financial dislocation and incipient crises. However, this success has not been a free good. Whereas profit-sustaining private investment leads to increases in productive capacity, profit-sustaining government deficits support consumption expenditures and defense spending—neither of which create resources. The combination of lender of last resort and massive government deficit in the aftermath of a crunch has succeeded in constraining debt deflations—but only at the price of setting the stage for inflations.

Conclusion

To the extent that financial crises occur and the Federal Reserve acts as a responsible lender of last resort when such events occur, the Federal Reserve cannot control the creation of high-powered or reserve money. To the extent that financial innovation leads to increases in the amount of financing available for any given reserve base and, inasmuch as the instruments created as a result of financial innovation act as a money asset, the Federal Reserve cannot control the money supply. The reaction of banks and other financial institutions in the aftermath of a crisis that triggers lender of last resort interventions can be characterized as setting up a structure of asset holdings that will enable these institutions to finance a subsequent inflationary expansion.

Once it is recognized that intervention is necessary to prevent a capitalist economy from intermittently degenerating into chaos, then it is possible to devise systems of intervention that are more efficient than our present system. My view is that we lucked out—the structure of big government and Federal Reserve actions that combined to prevent debt deflations and deep depressions after the midsixties was not consciously put in place to perform these functions. The system that ruled over the past 37 years was better in the whole than in its parts: No detail of what was in place in January 1981 was truly defensible *but* the totality was workable.

The tax bill of the summer of 1981 so compromised the revenue system that a surplus seems out of reach at any level of attainable real income. If inflation is to be contained, the tax and revenue system must be such that inflation leads to a surplus. This means that a modern level progressive income tax as well as the elimination of indexing from government spending are needed. Furthermore, government expenditures should be biased towards resource creation—including work programs—rather than support of consumption through transfer payments.

The principal function of central banking is to assure that financing is almost always available on terms that are consistent with the profits earned from using capital. This implies that the Federal Reserve should be more closely integrated into the financing of business than is true for a central bank whose assets are almost entirely government securities. We should once again try to move to a central bank-member bank structure in which a major part of central bank assets are of business-related paper. The discount window should be a normal functioning source of a significant portion of bank reserves. The use of the discount window and the borrower-lender relation this implies should enable the Federal Reserve to know more about financing developments than it now does.

It is necessary to remove the barriers to equity financing that exist in both the tax code and in the legacy of Glass-Steagle. Instead of moving to national branch banking, we should move towards banks that remain decentralized into local units but which no longer are barred from underwriting and dealing in equities.

Of course, given my perspective, any improvement that reform will bring will be transitory. As long as capitalism is entrepreneurial and innovative, it will have bouts of chaotic behavior.

Notes

1. Charles P. Kindleberger, in *Manias, Panics and Crashes* (New York: Basic Books, 1978), traces the Minsky view to John Stuart Mill, Alfred Marshall, Knut Wicksell, and Irving Fisher. Although I am not a Marxist scholar, it is, I believe, also found in the later Marxists, such as Rudolff Hilferding.

2. H. P. Minsky, *John Maynard Keynes* (New York: Columbia University Press, 1975).

3. My post-*John Maynard Keynes* view can be found in "Finance and Profits: The Changing Nature of American Business Cycles," in *The Business Cycle and Public Policy*, Joint Economic Committee Congress of the United States (Washington, D.C.; U.S. Government Printing Office, 1980), pp. 230–244.

"The Financial Instability Hypothesis: Capitalist Processes and the Behavior of the Economy," in *Financial Crises, Theory, History and Policy* C. P. Kindleberger and J. P. Laffarge (Cambridge, Eng.: Cambridge University Press; and Paris: Edition de la Maison des Sciences de l'Homme, 1982), pp. 13–381.

"Finance and Profits" and "The Financial Instability Hypothesis" are reprinted in *Can "It" Happen Again: Essays on Instability and Finance* (Armonk, New York: M.E. Sharpe, Inc., 1982).

4. M. Kalecki, *Selected Essays on the Dynamics of the Capitalist Economy* (Cambridge, Eng.: Cambridge University Press, 1971).

5. Henry C. Simons, "Rules vs. Authorities in Monetary Policy," *Journal of Political Economy* (1936), pp. 1–30.

John Maynard Keynes, *The General Theory of Employment, Interest and Money* (London: MacMillan, 1936).

6. Irving Fisher, "The Debt Deflation Theory of Great Depressions," *Econometrica* (1933), pp. 337–357.

Booms and Depressions, (New York: Adelphi Co., 1932).

100% Money, 3d Edition, (New Haven: The City Printing Co., 1945).

7. H. P. Minsky, "Monetary Systems and Accelerator Models," *A.E.R.* 47 (December, 1957). Reprinted in *Can "It" Happen Again.*

"A Linear Model of Cyclical Growth," *RESTAT* XLI, no. 2, (May 1959). Reprinted in *A.E.A. Readings in Business Cycles*, eds. R. A. Gordon and L. R. Klein Vol. X (Homewood, Ill. R. D. Irwin, 1965), pp. 79–99.

"The Integration of Simple Growth and Cycle Models," in *Patterns of Market Behavior: Essays in Honor of Philip Taft*, ed. M. J. Brennan (Providence R.I.: Brown University Press, 1965). Reprinted in *Can "It" Happen Again.*

8. R. Day, "Irregular Growth Cycles," *A.E.R.* (June 1982), 413.

9. F. H. Hahn, "Monetarism and Economic Theory," *Economica* 47 (February 1980), pp. 1–17.

K. J. Arrow and F. H. Hahn, *General Competitive Analysis* (San Francisco: Holden-Day, Inc., 1971).

10. H. P. Minsky, "Central Banking and Money Market Changes," *Q.J.E.* LXXI, no. 1 (May 1957), pp. 171–187. This perspective on central banking is not unlike L. W. Mints, *Monetary Policy for a Competitive Society* (New York: McGraw-Hill, 1950), and H. Simons, "Rules vs. Authorities in Monetary Policy." "Central Banking and Money Market Changes" is included in *Can "It" Happen Again.*

11. *Wall Street Journal*, July 15, 1982.

12. F. H. Hahn, "Reflections on the Invisible Hand," Fred Hirsch Memorial Lecture, University of Warwick, November 5, 1981 (mimeograph).

13. Geoff Harcourt, *Some Cambridge Controversies in the Theory of Capital* (Cambridge, Eng.: Cambridge University Press, 1972).

14. Starting from Smith, the standard theory's line might be Ricardo-Mill-Marshall/Walras-Hicks-Arrow-Debreu. The alternative line would be Smith-Ricardo-Marx-Keynes; the 70-year hiatus between Marx and Keynes in this line can be filled in by various Continental economists who wrote with an awareness of Marx that was largely absent in the British (and American) schools.

15. J. R. Hicks, "M. Keynes and the Classics, A Suggested Intrepretation," *Econometrica*, 1937.

16. In what follows, *banking* is used as a generic label for the various classes of dealers (position-takers) and brokers that intermediate and facilitate financing. Banking proper—i.e., organizations which have deposit subject to check among their liabilities—are referred to as either commercial or deposit banking.

17. Basil Moore, "The Endogenous Money Stock," *Journal of Post Keynesian Economics* II, no. 1 (Fall 1979).

18. H. P. Minsky, "Finance and Profits." Reprinted in H. P. Minsky, *Can "It" Happen Again*. See for a detailed exposition of the distinction among hedge, speculative, and Ponzi finance (pp. 22–23).

19. M. Kalecki, *Selected Essays*.

20. E. I. Altman, Statement Subcommittee on General Oversight, Committee on Small Business, House of Representatives, June 23, 1982.

DISCUSSION

Allan H. Meltzer

The more appropriate title for Minsky's paper might well be "Minsky's Stream of Consciousness on August 6." The paper touches on so many issues that it is not difficult to find some topics on which my judgments and Minsky's coincide and some on which they differ. This is an obvious advantage for a discussant who wishes to pick and choose, mixing a polite comment here with a slight growl there. The problem is that Minsky's ideas are presented in such a sketchy fashion that it is often difficult to be certain what he is trying to say.

An example is the lengthy, and for me, noninformative discussion of hedge, speculative, and Ponzi finance. I don't understand Minsky's distinction between the two last categories. Both types end with default on the principal. More basic is his failure to distinguish between expected and actual outcomes. Bankers, like the rest of us, draw their results from distributions. Some of their loans end in default and must be written off or worked out. With hindsight, it is easy to see that the price of oil is less likely to reach one hundred dollars a barrel in the next five years than many borrowers and lenders believed a few years ago. Perhaps estimates based on accelerating inflation will prove to be as foolish. Perhaps not. When major changes in relative prices or rates of inflation occur, we can expect to hear a great deal about bad judgment and risky loans.

What does this tell us about financial innovation? How did Penn Square innovate? Their failure seems to be an age-old story with differences confined to specific details. Did the loans to Poland lose their present value because some Ponzi scheme failed? Or is the problem with the Polish, Mexican, Penn Square loans, and many others that the lenders believed that governments and central banks would underwrite the failures, so the actual risk was perceived to be small. And, if the pleas for international and domestic bail-outs are answered, the taxpayers may yet have the privilege of sharing the losses or paying for all of them.

I am most certain about two issues, but my interest is piqued by an offhand remark, so I continue with what may be a digression or may be a restatement of Minsky's theme. Then I take up the two issues and the problem of instability in the current era.

What I take to be an offhand remark is Minsky's rumination about the "greed unleashed in 1981" by the Reagan administration. Minsky comments that this unleashing of greed produced an economic system in which "a Great Depression is possible." This statement conveys the idea that, before 1981, a major depression (or perhaps Major Depression) had become impossible. This would not be worth mentioning except that it is being said by the same Minsky who warned us repeatedly throughout the very same period that we were headed for another collapse.

The reason he changed his mind is obscure, but not more so than much of the rest of his message. I can reconstruct this much. Capitalism produces crises as a result of excessive expansion supported by credit and monetary expansion. The latter is caused, or perhaps abetted, by financial innovation. Institutional structure can prevent the crisis from occurring, and in recent years, two elements of the structure prevented crises. One is the size of government and the built-in stabilizers, particularly the rise in the deficit during recessions. The other is timely action by the lender of last resort.

Stripped of the language and obscurantisms that Minsky uses to convey his message, this is straight from the textbooks of the fifties and sixties. The message is that the private sector is unstable, but discretionary monetary and fiscal policy and built-in stabilizers keep recessions mild. Arthur Okun, surely a mainstream economist of the time, exulted at one point that in the 1960s the Commerce Department's monthly BCD had changed its name from *Business Cycle Digest* to *Business Conditions Digest* because of the success of policy.

What is it that has changed? The Reagan administration has not reduced the size of government and cannot be charged with eliminating deficits. The Administration and the Federal Reserve have just presided over an unprecedented series of mergers to prevent failures of a large number of depository institutions. It is true that the mergers are not lender of last resort loans. The lender of last resort lends to the market. It does not underwrite or share in the losses of insolvent institutions. Although the distinction is important, because the recent bail-outs encourage lenders to underprice future risks, it is not a distinction that Minsky makes.

I turn now to the first issue that I promised to address. Minsky writes that the Federal Reserve cannot control the money stock and serve as lender of last resort. This is why he suggests that our choice is either inflation or depression. His argument is incorrect, and his conclusion does not follow. The lender of last resort doesn't lose control of the money stock. The lender prevents a rapid decline in the money stock by providing base money or reserves to offset a decline in the money multiplier. The lender does not lose control of the money stock. He maintains control. In a fractional reserve banking system, a sudden increase in the demand for currency at many banks can be met if the lender of last resort increases the monetary base. This does not cause inflation. It prevents deflation or rapid disinflation.

The second issue I want to discuss is Minsky's proposal, at the end of his paper, that banks be permitted to hold equities. I am not opposed to banks buying any asset they wish, but I would not want to subsidize the risks by selling deposit insurance at a fixed price, as is now customary. The reason is that the bank's liabilities are fixed in nominal value. If a substantial part of a bank's assets are real assets, every price-level change has a heightened effect on the value of the bank. Banks that choose to take risks of this kind should be permitted to do so, provided the stockholders bear the residual risk and depositors are permitted to receive interest on their deposits to compensate for the risk they bear. Without these changes in regulatory practice, I see no merit in the proposal. It encourages banks to underestimate the risks they accept.

Minsky has been writing about financial instability for many years. His paper reminds us that he discussed some of these issues in 1957. Yet, to my knowledge, he has never produced a clearly stated hypothesis about the causes of instability or any evidence that would discriminate between various views.

The quarter century since 1957 is a not insignificant part of the economic history for which we have detailed and fairly accurate records. Most studies show this period to be the most stable period. Robert Gordon's computations of the standard deviation of departures from the trend growth rate of real output in the United States is 33 percent lower for the postwar years than any comparable period.[1] Until 1965, inflation remained low.

Postwar quarterly or annual variability of velocity is smaller than in prewar decades. Financial innovation has not produced either a substantial trend or a substantial change in trend from the fifties to the eighties. Nor is there any evidence that—despite the effects of controls, regulations, and inflation—velocity growth has become more variable. A most surprising fact about the trend growth of M1 velocity in the seventies, is that it is not significantly different from the growth rate experienced in the fifties.

There are, I believe, many ways in which stability can be increased and risk reduced. I cannot agree with Minsky that inflating is one of them. There is now considerable evidence of a positive association between the variability of inflation and the level of inflation. There is a growing body of evidence that inflation has real costs.[2] Minsky ignores all of this work.

There is no reason to be satisfied with the present level of risks or to ignore opportunities for improvement. High on my list of destabilizing financial practices are rules like Regulation Q, the nonpayment of interest on required reserves, differential reserve requirements, lag reserves accounting, and improper seasonal adjustment. During a period of inflation, many of these regulations increase fluctuations and variability. Does anyone doubt that the thrift industry would never have reached the position it did or that money market funds, offshore banking, and much of the rest of the so-called innovations would not have occurred if the regulations of the kind just cited had never been imposed? It is perhaps a fitting final comment on the level at which Minsky addresses the problem of instability that none of these regulations is mentioned.

Notes

1. Robert J. Gordon, "Price Inertia and Policy Ineffectiveness in the United States, 1890–1980," *Journal of Political Economy* 90 (December 1982), pp. 1087–1117.

2. Much of this evidence is discussed in Alex Cukierman, "Relative Price Variability and Inflation," Carnegie-Rochester Conference Series (forthcoming).

II EMPIRICAL IMPACT OF INNOVATION ON MEASUREMENT OF MONEY AND THE USE OF MONETARY TARGETS

3 FINANCIAL INNOVATIONS AND MEASUREMENT OF MONETARY AGGREGATES

Richard D. Porter and
Edward K. Offenbacher

The breakdown of the narrow inventory money demand specification in the mid-1970s has led to a reconsideration of the method by which monetary statistics are aggregated. Some have argued that the problem with the standard inventory demand specification lies in the proliferation of new "near money" substitutes, such as repurchase agreements (RPs) and money market mutual funds (MMMFs), in addition to new money market instruments created by legislation and by changes in regulation. Unfortunately, simply redefining the aggregates to be more inclusive—for example, replacing M1 with the sum of M1, RPs and MMMFs—does not reestablish a stable transactions demand function. In the face of such difficulties, some Board staff economists have advanced a new method of aggregation based on economic index numbers; see, for example, Barnett (1978, 1980, 1981, 1982, 1983); Barnett and Spindt (1982); Barnett, Spindt, and Offenbacher

The analyses and conclusions set forth are those of the authors and do not necessarily indicate concurrence by other members of the research staff, by the Board of Governors, or by Federal Reserve Banks. We wish to thank Amanda Bayer for research assistance and Mary Blackburn for expert typing. We also wish to thank Christian de Boissieu, Carol Corrado, Helen T. Farr, Marvin Goodfriend, Kenneth J. Kopecky, David Lindsey, Eileen Mauskopf, Paul Spindt, and Tom Simpson for comments on an earlier draft.

(1981); Offenbacher (1979, 1982a, 1982b); and Offenbacher and Porter (1982).

In applying index number theory to the monetary aggregates, it is assumed that monetary assets are durable goods held for the monetary services they provide over a finite period. Agents are assumed to trade off monetary services against interest yield. Thus, the opportunity cost of holding the asset is the foregone interest that could have been earned on the highest yielding asset, with the latter presumably offering no monetary services. In effect, the index number method assigns a user cost or rental price to each monetary asset to represent such opportunity costs, and uses standard index number procedures to combine components into an aggregate quantity index.

From the perspective of the transactions model, the use of index numbers will repair the problem of money demand to the extent that the problem derives from misspecifications of the opportunity costs (or of the way these costs enter the demand function). Because most empirical transactions demand specifications include, at most, three competing interest rates, it is conceivable that having all the rates represented in an index number would solve the money demand problem.

More importantly, because individual asset demand functions depend largely on their opportunity costs, combining assets with very different opportunity costs into a single simple sum aggregate will likely insure that such interest rate differentials show up in the behavior of the aggregate. The index number monetary aggregate, in contrast, appropriately compensates for these differential effects so that the resulting aggregate generally exhibits a more stable relationship with respect to an index of interest rates than the simple summation of these assets.[1]

However, index numbers which are based solely on opportunity cost interest rate differentials may not be a sufficiently general way to deal with the other major explanation for the downward shift in the demand for M1—improvements in money management techniques that have come about as a result of lowered real transactions costs. For example, as information processing costs have fallen, it has become cheaper for firms to gather information about their short-run stochastic cash flows, thus reducing the conditional variance of such cash flows. The firm is thus able to carry on the same level of transactions with a smaller inventory of demand deposits to cover stochastic flows. Such technical progress will not necessarily be picked up with *existing* index number procedures, which take only the interest rate differentials and not these transactions costs into account.

In the present paper, we consider both the decline in transactions costs and the use of index numbers. In the next section, we review the performance of the standard demand for money equation and briefly consider the only empirical transactions model that has sought to resolve the money demand problem by incorporating a cash management option—the Porter-Simpson model. We then explore in some detail various indirect measures of transactions costs and their ability to explain the shortfall in deposit growth. While our conclusions about the usefulness of the transactions costs approach in explaining the demand deposit puzzle are still quite tentative since the full analysis of the approach has not been completed, the method does appear to have some promise. The third section discusses the index number approach to monetary aggregation focusing on the divisia index in the context of a multiasset inventory demand model. We show that, in such a framework, index number aggregates lead to a remarkably better aggregate demand specification than conventional simple sum aggregation. The empirical comparisons of conventional and divisia aggregates that are presented in this section tend to support this theoretical presumption: results for the index number aggregates that include M1 and transactions-oriented near monies such as MMMFs, overnight RPs, and overnight Eurodollars are decidedly superior to the conventional sum aggregates.

Finally, the concluding section seeks to reconcile the transactions cost and index number approaches. We suggest the need for a generalization of the existing index number method if and when hard data on transactions costs become readily available.

The M1 Breakdown Once More: A Look at the Brokerage Fee

Recent Errors in Goldfeld's M1 Specification

Until about 1974, a large body of evidence had accumulated suggesting that a stable demand function for M1 existed for the United States specified along the lines of equation 3.1:

$$\ln\left(\frac{m^d}{P}\right)_t = a_0 + a_1\ln(r_{1t}) + a_2\ln(r_{2t}) + a_3\ln(y_t) + a_4\ln\left(\frac{m}{P}\right)_{t-1} \tag{3.1}$$

where m^d = demand for money

r_{1t} = short-term, nominal, open market interest rate

r_{2t} = short-term, nominal, regulated interest rate
y = real output or income
p = price level.

Goldfeld (1973) compared the various empirical approaches to the demand for money and concluded that equation 3.1 showed the most stability.

Starting in about mid-1974, however, this formulation as well as most variants of it persistently overpredicted the growth rate of the money stock. Using the particular representations of the model estimated in appendix table A–1 [Goldfeld, 1973], table 3–1 presents the cumulative percentage overprediction error when this equation is dynamically simulated over two subperiods: 1967:1 to 1974:2 and 1974:3 to 1981:4. The error is measured relative to an adjusted M1 concept.[2] While the equation tends to drift off for a few quarters in the early period, the errors never run up significantly. Over the early period, the average out-of-sample error was a negligible .35 percent with a root mean square error of 1.1 percent on annual changes and a maximum annual error of 1.7 percent in 1969. By contrast, over the period from mid-1974 to 1981:4, the error cumulates to over 22 percent. On an annual basis, the error in predicting fourth quarter to fourth quarter growth rates averaged 2.6 percent with a root mean square error of 3.3 percent. In 1981 alone, the increase in the error in the adjusted M1 measure was 6.7 percent.

Improved Money Management Techniques Have Contributed to the Breakdown

A considerable body of work has emerged in the past seven years trying to explain this breakdown in the standard inventory demand equation.[3] None of this subsequent work has led to a successful respecification of the demand function for the latter period which achieves the degree of stability evident in the early period in either the Goldfeld equation or any of its variants. The conclusion reached by several Board staff members is that the major source of the shift is technological; see, for example, Porter, Simpson, and Mauskopf (1979); Mauskopf and Porter (1979); Simpson (1979); Simpson and Porter (1980); and Offenbacher (1982b). It appears that in the face of persistently high opportunity costs of holding money, deposit holders have sought to improve their money management techniques—thus endogenous technological progress in cash management has taken place. These developments have also been strengthened by improvements in computer and telecommunications technology and the development of various cash

Table 3-1. Out-of-Sample Errors from a Goldfeld M1 Equation for 1967:1 to 1974:2 and for 1974:3 to 1981:4[a]

Date	*Cumulative Percentage Error*	*Annual Growth Rate Errors*	*Date*	*Cumulative Percentage Error*	*Annual Growth Rate Errors*
1967:1	−.2		1974:3	1.2	
:2	−.3		:4	3.0	
:3	−1.0				
:4	−1.0	−1.1	1975:1	5.1	
			:2	5.4	
1968:1	−.8		:3	5.9	
:2	−.9		:4	7.6	4.8
:3	−1.5				
:4	−1.9	−.9	1976:1	7.8	
			:2	7.5	
1969:1	−2.3		:3	8.2	
:2	−1.6		:4	8.6	.9
:3	−.5				
:4	−.3	1.7	1977:1	8.3	
			:2	8.9	
1970:1	−.1		:3	9.2	
:2	.1		:4	8.9	.3
:3	−.2				
:4	−.1	.2	1978:1	8.5	
			:2	9.4	
1971:1	.9		:3	9.9	
:2	.8		:4	10.6	1.7
:3	.4				
:4	1.2	1.4	1979:1	11.9	
			:2	11.7	
1972:1	1.7		:3	11.5	
:2	1.7		:4	11.9	1.2
:3	1.2				
:4	.5	−.8	1980:1	12.6	
			:2	16.3	
1973:1	.2		:3	15.3	
:2	.7		:4	14.8	2.8
:3	.7				
:4	.7	1.0	1981:1	18.0	
			:2	18.1	
1974:1	1.4		:3	20.8	
:2	2.6		:4	22.1	6.4

(*Continued*)

Table 3-1 (*Continued*)

	Annualized Quarterly Growth Rates	*Annual Growth Rates*	*Annualized Quarterly Growth Rates*	*Annual Growth Rates*
Mean Error	.4	.2	2.6	2.6
Root Mean Square Error	2.1	1.1	4.7	3.3

[a]Error defined as predicted minus actual. M1 based on adjusted concept; see footnote 2 in the text.

management procedures, such as cash concentration, sweep accounts, and remote disbursing.[4]

Table 3–2 reports some simulation results for a variant of equation 3.1—the Porter-Simpson equation—which adds a cash management option to the standard inventory model.[5] Empirically, this equation augments a standard money demand specification, such as equation 3.1, with an interest rate ratchet variable which enters the equation with an elasticity that increases (in absolute value) with the level of the ratchet variable.[6] As intermediate term rates rise above a moving average of previous rates, deposit holders are induced to undertake the fixed costs of improving their money management techniques. In general, such improvements will result in more responsive money demand with respect to changes in short-term interest rates and a lowered response with respect to changes in output. These effects are crudely proxied by postulating that the elasticity of the ratchet variable increases (in absolute value) with the level of the ratchet. While the out-of-sample simulation results still lack stability, they do track growth rates fairly accurately since 1975, particularly when measured on an annual (fourth quarter to fourth quarter) basis.

There are, however, a number of difficulties with this equation. In effect, it treats all of the cash management improvements as an endogenous consequence of the high interest rates, whereas improvements may be more closely related to developments in and pricing of information processing, telecommunications, and so forth. Second, though the nonconstant elasticity has a basis in theory, the functional form has an arbitrary element. As the ratchet rises, predictions will be made with values of this regressor necessarily outside of its historical range. While the predictions have been reasonably accurate to date, we cannot be confident that this particular functional form will hold up. The problem is simply that there are any

Table 3-2. Out-of-Sample Errors from the Porter-Simpson M1 Equation[a]

Date	*Cumulative Percentage Error*	*Annual Growth Rate Errors*	*Date*	*Cumulative Percentage Error*	*Annual Growth Rate Errors*
1974:3	.69		1978:1	5.72	
:4	1.39		:2	6.21	
			:3	6.46	
1975:1	2.84		:4	7.04	.68
:2	2.93				
:3	3.15		1979:1	7.87	
:4	4.49	3.21	:2	7.10	
			:3	6.49	
1976:1	4.56		:4	6.48	−.56
:2	4.60				
:3	5.58		1980:1	5.88	
:4	5.54	1.08	:2	7.83	
			:3	6.47	
1977:1	5.10		:4	6.13	−.35
:2	5.83				
:3	6.55		1981:1	8.33	
:4	6.37	.85	:2	6.09	
			:3	6.72	
			:4	6.89	.73
			Mean Error		.81
			Root Mean Square Error		1.40

[a]Error defined as predicted minus actual. M1 based on adjusted concept; see footnote 2 in the text.

number of functional forms with increasing elasticities, and all that this one has to recommend it is that it has worked reasonably well thus far.

The Transactions Demand for Money with Estimates of Brokerage Fees

In the remainder of this section, we explore a series of alternatives to the Porter-Simpson empirical specification. We remain within the transactions framework, but seek to resolve the breakdown by *indirectly* estimating the brokerage fee that theory suggests belongs in the transactions demand function. The term brokerage fee is used loosely to cover all the various costs involved in the process of cash management. In the simplest case, the brokerage fee represents simply the fixed cost of converting an interest-bearing asset into cash or cash into an interest-bearing asset. If the alternative is a passbook savings account, the costs are "shoe leather" and the value of time in making trips to the bank. More generally, brokerage fee is meant to include, in addition to explicit per-transfer costs, personnel costs, the costs of wire transfers, computer software and hardware, and so forth. Owing to a paucity of data concerning the brokerage fee, in the usual empirical framework it is assumed to be constant over time and thus subsumed in the intercept.[7] However, a number of cash management improvements have come as the result of a fall in real brokerage fees or transactions costs.

All our indirect estimates of the brokerage fee exploit the relationship in standard transactions models between a measure of debits to demand deposit accounts and the arguments of the money demand function. Specifically, the standard Miller-Orr transactions model suggests that expected money balances and expected financial debits to demand deposit accounts have the same determinants. In the Miller-Orr model, it can be readily shown that[8]

$$m = \alpha_{1h} \left(\frac{by^2}{r} \right)^{1/h} \tag{3.2}$$

$$d = \alpha_{2h} \left(\frac{ry^4}{b} \right)^{1/h} \tag{3.3}$$

where m = average (steady state) money balances

y = the standard deviation of cash flows

r = opportunity cost of holding m

b = brokerage fee in nominal terms

d = financial debits, the average (steady state) dollar volume of transactions in demand deposits that are generated by purchasing the nonmonetary asset, which is the interest-bearing alternative to demand deposits

h = 3 in Miller-Orr model

α_{ih} = constants of proportionality.

Note that interest rates and the brokerage fee have the opposite signs in the two equations. An increase in interest rates will raise expected financial debits but lower average money balances. On the other hand, a decrease in brokerage fees will lower deposit holdings but increase expected financial debits. Finally, financial turnover can be determined from equations 3.2 and 3.3 as

$$t = d/m = \alpha_{3h} \left(\frac{yr}{b}\right)^{2/h} \tag{3.4}$$

where $\alpha_{3h} = \alpha_{2h}/\alpha_{1h}$.

Similar results are also obtained in the deterministic Baumol-Tobin model; see Porter (1976).

It must be admitted at the outset that no empirical series on financial debits exists that matches the concept of d defined above. The problem is not so much separating financial transactions from nonfinancial, though clearly that is not a trivial matter, but that any measure of financial transactions is bound to include transactions besides those that represent purchases of the interest-bearing alternative to money. For example, money changing transactions—debiting the demand account to obtain cash—should in principle be excluded from this measure of financial transactions. If the empirical results presented below have any validity, it must be assumed that these other transactions are positively correlated with the concept of financial transactions required in the transactions model. That is, brokerage fees on these different types of financial transactions must be positively correlated.[9]

Another objection to the use of debits data is that there is virtually no economic limit to the gross amount of debits that may be generated. Imagine, for the sake of argument, that two individuals with demand deposit accounts in different banks were increasing debits without limit by continuously exchanging balances between their respective accounts. If there are no transactions costs, what incentive do they have to limit the process? The answer is that they would not generally receive good funds immediately, but would have to wait for a few days. Thus, there is an opportunity cost involved in the exchange even if there were free checking on both accounts. And, if wire transfers were used to obtain good funds immediately, an explicit transfer cost would be incurred.

Estimates and Simulations in Linear Specificiations

The simplest and, as will be shown, most controversial way of obtaining a brokerage fee series is to solve for b using equation 3.4 with $h = 3$:

Table 3-3. Money Demand Estimates for Demand Deposits with Alternative Representations of Brokerage Variable[a]

			Independent Variables			
Row	*Equation Variable*	*Constant*	*Treasury Bill Rate*	*GNP NSA*	*Brokerage Fee or Debits*	*Lagged Dependent Variable*
1	Brokerage fee based on turnover	.034 (.1)	−.056 (−8.5)	.175 (13.0)	.034 (6.4)	.803 (16.8)
2	Brokerage fee based on turnover	.199 (1.2)	−.066 (−10.9)	.213 (9.6)	.047 (8.4)	.725 (17.9)
3	Brokerage fee based on financial debits	.015 (.1)	−.037 (−9.0)	.123 (13.3)	.014 (6.5)	.883 (19.0)
4	Brokerage fee based on financial debits	−.108 (−1.2)	−.039 (−10.1)	.121 (8.5)	.017 (7.0)	.911 (40.4)
5	Financial debits (replaces brokerage fee)	.015 (.1)	−.023 (−6.7)	.179 (12.1)	−.042 (−6.5)	.884 (19.0)
6	Financial debits (replaces brokerage fee)	−.108 (−1.2)	−.022 (−7.1)	.187 (8.1)	−.050 (−7.0)	.911 (40.0)
7	Standard specification	−.082 (−.2)	−.021 (−5.6)	.185 (13.1)	—	.808 (13.5)
8	Standard specification	−.170 (−1.3)	−.022 (−6.3)	.029 (3.4)	—	1.01 (40.6)

[a]Uses *adjusted* concept of demand deposits; see footnote 2 in the text. T-ratios are shown in parentheses beneath the estimated coefficients.

$$b^{(t)} = (r^2 y^2 / t^3)^{1/2}$$

The resulting brokerage fee estimate can then be substituted into an empirical money demand function[10]

$$\ln(m/p) = a_0 + a_1 \ln(r) + a_2 \ln(y) + a_3 \ln(b^{(t)}/p) + a_4 \ln(m/p)_{-1} \tag{3.5}$$

	Summary Statistics						
		Standard	AR(4) Coefficients				
Period of Fit	$\bar{R}^2$	Error Estimates	$\rho1$	$\rho2$	$\rho3$	$\rho4$	Durbin-Watson
55:1–74:2	.979	.00675	.42 (3.8)	−.55 (−4.8)	.33 (2.9)	.35 (3.2)	1.80
55:1–81:4	.967	.00942	.18 (2.0)	−.23 (−2.1)	.15 (1.6)	.49 (5.5)	2.10
55:1–74:2	.978	.00689	.35 (3.1)	−.59 (−2.6)	.26 (2.3)	.30 (2.7)	1.78
55:1–81:4	.964	.00976	−.06 (−.6)	−.35 (−1.7)	−.04 (−.5)	.40 (4.2)	2.08
55:1–74:2	.978	.00689	.35 (3.1)	−.38 (−2.4)	.26 (2.3)	.30 (2.7)	1.78
55:1–81:4	.964	.00976	−.06 (−.6)	−.44 (−1.4)	−.04 (−.5)	.40 (4.2)	2.08
55:1–74:2	.976	.00721	.64 (5.7)	−.73 (−2.2)	.52 (4.5)	.35 (3.3)	1.76
55:1–81:4	.955	.0110	−.12 (−1.7)	−.24 (−1.3)	−.10 (−1.4)	.66 (9.1)	2.00

The results from such money-demand regressions are reported in rows 1 and 2 of table 3–3 and table 3–4 for two dependent variables, the demand deposit component of the money supply (DDCMS) (table 3–3) and nonfinancial business demand deposits (NFBDD) as measured in the quarterly demand deposit ownership survey (DDOS) (table 3–4). The dependent variables were selected because previous work has established

Table 3-4. Money Demand Estimates for Nonfinancial Business Deposits with Alternative Representations of Brokerage Variable

			Independent Variables		
Row	*Equation Variable*	*Constant*	*Treasury Bill Rate*	*GNP NSA*	*Brokerage Fee or Debits*
1	Brokerage fee based on turnover	6.86 (23.3)	−.122 (−7.1)	.768 (14.9)	.171 (9.3)
2	Brokerage fee based on turnover	6.84 (26.4)	−.121 (−6.8)	.761 (17.2)	.193 (14.9)
3	Brokerage fee based on turnover	6.68 (19.8)	−.187 (−6.4)	.798 (13.8)	.215 (7.2)
4	Brokerage fee based on turnover	6.83 (21.8)	−.192 (−11.8)	.772 (14.3)	.220 (13.9)
5	Brokerage fee based on financial debits	10.96 (15.7)	−.048 (−2.4)	.198 (1.9)	.145 (5.7)
6	Brokerage fee based on financial debits	9.99 (32.0)	−.025 (−1.3)	.337 (6.9)	.112 (10.6)
7	Brokerage fee based on financial debits	10.25 (26.4)	−.070 (−3.4)	.315 (5.1)	.126 (9.2)
8	Brokerage fee based on financial debits	10.76 (25.4)	−.100 (−4.8)	.246 (3.6)	.139 (10.5)
9	Financial debits	10.96 (15.7)	.097 (3.8)	.779 (18.5)	−.436 (−5.7)
10	Financial debits	10.76 (25.4)	.040 (1.5)	.803 (14.3)	−.418 (−10.5)
11	Standard specification	7.13 (23.2)	.008 (.36)	.782 (14.3)	—
12	Standard specification	6.51 (21.1)	.021 (.82)	.783 (17.7)	—
13	Standard specification	5.92 (15.7)	.007 (.32)	.85 (15.4)	—
14	Standard specification	5.18 (11.3)	-6.8×10^{-4} (−.02)	.880 (16.9)	—

Note: t-ratios are shown in parentheses beneath the estimated coefficients.

Period of Fit	$\bar{R}^2$	Standard Error Estimates	AR(4) Coefficients ρ1	ρ2	ρ3	ρ4	Durbin-Watson
			Summary Statistics				
71:3–75:4	.935	.0118	.51 (2.2)	−.53 (−2.2)	.23 (.9)	.19 (.9)	2.00
71:3–77:4	.905	.0152	.57 (2.8)	−.75 (−2.9)	.35 (1.2)	.04 (.2)	2.04
71:3–79:4	.839	.0194	.60 (3.4)	−.28 (−1.5)	.40 (2.1)	−.01 (−.1)	2.01
71:3–81:4	.938	.0188	.56 (3.6)	−.38 (−2.3)	.38 (2.1)	.11 (.7)	1.98
71:3–75:4	.925	.0128	.80 (3.9)	−.67 (−3.0)	.50 (2.1)	.04 (.2)	2.15
71:3–77:4	.901	.0156	.70 (3.4)	−.74 (−3.4)	.52 (1.9)	.01 (.0)	1.98
71:3–79:4	.849	.0188	.56 (3.3)	−.32 (−1.8)	.39 (2.1)	−.03 (−.2)	2.12
71:3–81:4	.913	.0223	.70 (4.4)	−.41 (−2.2)	.43 (2.2)	−.04 (−.3)	2.03
71:3–75:4	.925	.0128	.80 (3.9)	−.67 (−3.0)	.50 (2.1)	.04 (.2)	2.15
71:3–81:4	.913	.0223	.70 (4.4)	−.41 (−2.2)	.43 (2.2)	−.04 (−.3)	2.03
71:3–75:4	.891	.0153	.89 (3.6)	−.44 (−1.4)	.45 (1.4)	.17 (.7)	1.80
71:3–77:4	.865	.0182	.97 (4.1)	−.73 (−2.2)	.71 (2.1)	.03 (.10)	1.76
71:3–79:4	.856	.0183	.64 (3.6)	−.24 (−1.3)	.50 (2.6)	.07 (.38)	1.90
71:3–81:4	.903	.0235	.98 (6.1)	−.45 (−2.2)	.56 (2.7)	−.10 (−.63)	2.00

that the shortfall in demand deposits is concentrated in the demand deposit component of M1, particularly in holdings of nonfinancial businesses [Farr, Pruitt, and Porter, 1979]. With a minor exception, Cramer's method (1980) for constructing a nonfinancial debits series was followed.[11] Financial debits were then estimated as the difference between an estimate of total debits and nonfinancial debits. To abstract from problems of seasonal adjustment, not seasonally adjusted series for nominal GNP (y), demand deposits (m), were used in the regression along with treasury bill rates (r).[12]

The regression results for this simple brokerage fee specification are highly encouraging. The variables all enter with the correct sign and have highly significant t-ratios. The long-run elasticities for the demand deposit equation (table 3–3) are roughly the same in the two periods with elasticities of −.28 and −.24, .89 and .77, and .17 and .17 for r, y, and b in the shorter and longer periods, respectively. By contrast, the long-run coefficients of the standard specification—rows 7 and 8 of table 3–3—are inadmissible over the longer sample period. Further, the results from the standard specification for nonfinancial business deposit holdings—rows 11–14 of table 3–4—have incorrect signs on the interest rate variable. Moreover, for both deposit measures, the specification has a higher standard error than the specification which includes the brokerage fee. Finally, the NFBDD regressions which include the brokerage term show a much greater degree of stability as the sample period is extended from the midseventies to the early eighties than those that exclude it.

The absence of any lagged terms in the NFBDD results distinguishes from these estimates most quarterly money demand equations. Lagged terms, represented either by using a lagged dependent variable or, alternatively, by incorporating explicit lags for the right-hand-side variable, were not statistically significant when added to the NFBDD equations. Of course, the presence of a lagged dependent variable in a transactions model does not have a firm basis in theory. If brokerage costs tend to be fixed—that is, independent of the size of the transaction—then it pays to adjust all at once when cash balances have reached either an upper limit or a lower limit, rather than incur fixed costs gradually as in the partial adjustment specification. Because we believe most of the costs of managing the narrow aggregates tend to be of a fixed nature, lagged dependent variables cannot be rationalized by the partial adjustments specification.

A lagged dependent variable may also be present if there is uncertainty about the movements in income and interest rates or errors in measurement in these variables even though the true structural demand relationship has no lags. If, for example, an upward movement in interest rates is thought to be transitory, it may not pay to incur the transactions costs of moving out of money and into an interest-bearing substitute. This signal extraction problem could lead to estimated distributed lags in interest rates and income or to lagged dependent variables [see Goodfriend (1982a)]. Alternatively, if the variance of the measurement error in income or interest rates increases, the lagged dependent variable will increase.[13] We believe that such measurement errors contaminate several money demand specifications.

For the demand deposit component of M1 (table 3–3), lagged terms are apparently required. Furthermore, the lagged dependent variable in these regressions are, in our opinion, implausibly large. Using the $b^{(t)}$ brokerage series,[14] disaggregated money demand regressions of the form of equation 3.5 for the household category in the DDOS data and remaining DDOS deposits (total deposits less nonfinancial business deposits and household deposits) indicate that the lags are only present in the household regressions. The source of these effects is not apparent to us. It could reflect measurement error in the brokerage fee which is more significant for households than other deposit holders.

Remarkable out-of-sample results for the first equation in table 3–3 are reported in the left-hand panel of table 3–5. Over the difficult post-mid-1974 period, the equation exhibits no drift (mean error) at all and the root mean square error on fourth quarter to fourth quarter growth rates is about 1 percent.

Because the brokerage series itself depends on demand deposits—having been constructed as a function of turnover where turnover depends on demand deposits—there may be some suspicion of circularity in these results.[15] Such an objection can be overcome by considering the alternative brokerage series implicitly defined in equation 3.3, namely

$$b^{(d)} = \left(\frac{\alpha_{2h}}{d}\right)^h ry^4 \tag{3.6}$$

That is, money holdings are given by an *empirical* money demand function of the form

$$\ln(m/p) = a_0 + a_1\ln(r) + a_2\ln(y) + a_3\ln(b^{(d)}/p) + a_4\ln(m/p)_{-1} \tag{3.7}$$

As before, we assume that the a's are parameters which do not satisfy the theoretical restrictions in equation 3.2 exactly. Table 3–3, rows 3 and 4, displays the results of such a regression for $h = 3$, the Miller-Orr elasticity value, as well for an alternative specification in which *real financial debits*, rows 5 and 6, are used in place of the brokerage fee term. That is

$$\ln(m/p) = b_0 + b_1\ln(r) + b_2\ln(y) + b_3\ln(d/p) + b_4\ln(m/p)_{-1} \tag{3.8}$$

Table 3-5. Postsample Errors from a Dynamic Simulation of Alternative Money Demand Equations for the Demand Deposit Component of M1[a]

	Brokerage Fee Based on Turnover		*Brokerage Fee Based on Financial Debits OR Financial Debits Directly*		*Standard Specification*	
Date	*Cumulative Percentage Error*	*Annual Growth Rate Errors*	*Cumulative Percentage Error*	*Annual Growth Rate Errors*	*Cumulative Percentage Error*	*Annual Growth Rate Errors*
1974:3	.5		.6		.9	
:4	1.2		1.6		2.3	
1975:1	3.5		4.2		4.9	
:2	2.3		3.1		3.8	
:3	1.9		2.7		3.5	
:4	3.2	2.0	4.2	2.6	5.1	2.8
1976:1	4.3		5.4		6.5	
:2	3.4		4.5		5.7	
:3	3.8		5.1		6.5	
:4	3.6	.4	5.1	1.0	6.8	1.7
1977:1	4.5		6.2		8.1	
:2	4.1		6.0		8.2	
:3	4.5		6.4		8.8	
:4	3.9	.3	6.0	.9	8.6	1.8

1978:1	5.3		7.5		10.2	
:2	5.2		7.4		10.4	
:3	5.1		7.5		10.9	
:4	5.5	1.6	8.0	2.0	11.6	3.0
1979:1	8.6		11.4		15.5	
:2	6.6		9.6		14.1	
:3	5.0		8.2		13.6	
:4	4.6	−.9	7.9	−.1	14.0	2.2
1980:1	5.9		9.4		16.7	
:2	8.4		12.4		20.7	
:3	5.4		9.6		18.7	
:4	3.0	−1.6	7.1	−.7	17.2	3.0
1981:1	6.1		10.9		22.6	
:2	3.7		8.9		21.7	
:3	3.7		9.6		24.3	
:4	2.8	−.3	9.1	1.8	25.0	6.7
Mean Error		.23		1.06		3.04
Root Mean Square Error		1.22		1.52		3.42

[a]Based on equations for demand deposit component of M1 in table 3–3. Error defined as predicted minus actual. Deposits measured with respect to our adjusted concept; see footnote 2 in the text.

Notice first that the real financial debits term enters the regression with a negative sign. Given the theoretical negative relationship between debits and the brokerage fee in equation 3.3, it is this feature of the data that produces the positive brokerage fee elasticity in the equation 3.7 regressions. Also observe that the standard errors in the two equations are identical. It is easy to show that this latter result is no accident, as the least-squares projections in the two cases must be the same; that is, equations 3.7 and 3.8 must necessarily produce the same in-sample and out-of-sample predictions.[16]

While the out-of-sample simulations of the DDCMS equation reported in the middle panel of table 3–5 are not as accurate as the equations using the brokerage series derived from turnover, they still represent a considerable improvement over the standard transactions equation for demand deposits, shown in the right-hand panel of table 3–5.

Though the projections or predictions from equations 3.6 and 3.7 are mathematically identical, the structural money demand parameters are not necessarily defined by the estimates for equation 3.7 which use a brokerage fee. Recall that we have implicitly let $h = 3$ in obtaining the $b^{(d)}$ series used in equation 3.7. However, no restrictions were put on the demand equation 3.7 when it was estimated. Our procedure can be rationalized by assuming that equation 3.3 holds exactly with $h = 3$, but that equation 3.2 is more general, for instance

$$m = \alpha_{1h} r^{(-1/h_2)} y^{[1-(1/h_1)]} b^{(1/h_1)} \tag{3.9}$$

The former assumption can be justified on the grounds that businesses generate most of the debits in the system, and the Miller-Orr model applies to them. The equivalence between the two projections above remains valid in this case as well. Nonetheless, unless we assume that h does equal 3 (the Miller-Orr case), the structural estimation of the money demand parameters is not determinate. It turns out that, in the more general case, a nonlinear procedure is required to obtain estimates of the parameters.

A Nonlinear Specification

So far we have relied on linear regression techniques to estimate money demand equations under the implicit assumption that there is no error term in the debits equation. However, the omission of this error term cannot be justified. It is likely that the error term in the debits equation has a bigger variance than the error term in the demand equation. If the equation contains an error term, then solving for the brokerage fee as we have done ignores the implicit errors-in-variables problem. In addition, the linear approach may not be practical for real world forecasting purposes if financial debits cannot be forecasted with some accuracy. Finally, the consistency of the linear model requires that the parameters in the debits equation be known exactly, but lets the money demand parameters be free.

An approach which deals squarely with each of these problems and which also jointly estimates equations 3.2 and 3.3 directly is to postulate a third equation that determines the brokerage fee. Suppose, for example,

$$\ln (b_t/p_t) = \beta_0 + \beta_1 x_{1t} + \beta_2 x_{2t} + \ldots + \beta_k x_{kt} + \varepsilon_{1t} \qquad (3.10)$$

where x_{it} = ith determinant of b_t

ε_t = residual error term

Given a choice for the r.h.s. of equation 3.10, it can be estimated jointly with the money demand and debits functions

$$\ln(m_t/p_t) = \gamma_0 + \gamma_1 \ln(r_t) + \gamma_2 \ln(y_t/p_t) + \gamma_3 \ln(b_t/p_t) + \gamma_4 \ln(m/p)_{t-1} + \varepsilon_{2t} \qquad (3.11)$$

$$\ln(d_t) = \delta_0 + \delta_1 \ln(r_t) + \delta_2 \ln(y_t) + \delta_3 \ln(b_t) + \delta_4 \ln(d_{t-1}) + \varepsilon_{3t} \qquad (3.12)$$

In the three-equation system consisting of equations 3.10 to 3.12, the variable b_t is viewed as an unobserved variable. A variant of a maximum likelihood technique advanced by Goldberger (1972) may be employed to estimate this system.

Divisia Aggregation

In addition to the technological improvements that thave enabled individuals to economize on cash balances, financial innovation has also taken the form of an increase in the variety of financial assets that have some monetary attributes. These assets contribute to both the store-of-wealth function and the monetary function in varying proportions. This raises the question of whether conventional sum aggregation, which gives equal weight to equal amounts of any two assets, is an appropriate procedure for capturing the contributions of the various assets to the monetary function. An alternative means of aggregation, one which assigns a weight to each asset based on the opportunity cost of holding that asset, has been developed at the Federal Reserve Board by William Barnett, Edward Offenbacher, and Paul Spindt. The new aggregates are called divisia monetary aggregates since the aggregation formula used is the divisa index number formula. The basic motivation for these aggregates is an attempt to separate the monetary services from the pure store of wealth function and to aggregate only over the monetary services. The remainder of this section is organized as follows. The first subsection briefly presents the divisia aggregates; the next subsection shows that divisia aggregation is more reasonable than conventional aggregation if the underlying component quantities are determined by an inventory-theoretic approach. Finally, empirical comparisons of conventional and divisia aggregates are presented. The results favor divisia aggregation for aggregates that include M1 and transactions-oriented near monies such as MMMFs, overnight RPs and overnight Eurodollars. We conclude that if an aggregate comprised of these components is to be used in a given analysis, the divisia method of aggregation is highly recommended.

Divisia Monetary Aggregates

The application of divisia aggregation to monetary assets is designed to obtain an empirically tractable means of distinguishing between the monetary and the nonmonetary functions of these assets. Any asset or durable good is, by its very existence, a store of wealth, and it may or may not provide other services. The store of wealth function of an asset is its ability to serve as a vehicle for transferring consumption from a given period into the future. Casual observation suggests that financial assets generally provide some combination of monetary and store-of-wealth services.[17] Thus, as an empirical simplification it appears reasonable to assume that financial assets provide only these two services. The problem is how to distinguish between them empirically. The approach adopted here is to obtain a measure of the value of only the monetary services provided by a dollar of each financial asset that is designated as a component of a given aggregate. The aggregation procedure uses both these value measures and the dollar volumes of each asset.

In general, economic theory suggests that in order to obtain an aggregate measure of quantity for a bundle of different goods, the quantities of the components should be weighted by some function of their opportunity costs. For example, a measure of the quantity of fruit can be obtained by combining data on the quantities of apples and oranges, provided that the method of combination makes judicious use of the prices of apples and oranges. Thus, in order to obtain a measure of the quantity of the monetary services provided by a group of different financial assets, we require a set of measures of the opportunity cost of only the monetary services provided by each asset. Suppose we assume that each financial asset to be included in a given monetary aggregate provides only store of wealth and monetary services, and suppose we also assume that the value of a given asset's store of wealth service can be measured adequately by the return on that asset. Finally, suppose that one asset can be treated as a pure store of wealth, providing no monetary services. Clearly such an asset will pay a higher return than any asset that also provides monetary services. In practice, the pure store of wealth, or benchmark, asset is taken to be the asset with the highest return. Given these assumptions, the opportunity cost of obtaining the monetary services from the assets that do provide them can be measured as the interest foregone by not holding the benchmark asset. Operationally, the opportunity costs, also called the user costs of monetary services, are calculated as simple interest differentials.[18]

The assumption that only the return on an asset adequately measures its value as a store of wealth is somewhat less reasonable than the assumption that financial assets provide only the two services discussed. Differences in asset yields may be due to factors that are not clearly monetary in nature, such as term to maturity and portfolio risk. The issues involved in dealing with these factors are quite complicated and have been discussed elsewhere at length.[19] The upshot is that an adjustment for maturity differences is made in constructing the monetary service user costs, but no adjustment is made for risk.

Having constructed the user costs, one can construct divisia monetary quantity and user cost indexes.[20] The formula for the divisia quantity index, denoted Q_t (in discrete time) is[21]

$$\log Q_t - \log Q_{t-1} = \sum_i w_{it}^* \log (q_{it}/q_{i,t-1}) \tag{3.13}$$

where

$$w_{it}^* = \frac{1}{2}\left(\frac{p_{it}q_{it}}{\sum p_{it}q_{it}} + \frac{p_{i,t-1}q_{i,t-1}}{\sum p_{i,t-1}q_{i,t-1}}\right)$$

with p_{it} and q_{it} denoting the user cost and dollar volumes of the ith asset.

Divisia Aggregation in a Transactions Framework

This subsection shows that divisia aggregation is considerably more reasonable than conventional sum aggregation under the assumption that the demands for monetary assets are determined in an inventory theoretic framework. Let q_i and p_i represent the quantity and user cost of the ith monetary asset with $i = 1, \ldots, N$. Let b_i denote the brokerage cost of a single transaction in asset i, and Y denote a scale variable. The two most popular inventory-theoretic approaches to the transactions demand for money are the Baumol-Tobin model, which is deterministic, and the Miller-Orr model, which assumes a stochastic cash flow. The multiasset versions of both of these models yield double logarithmic demand specifications where the log of real balances of each asset is expressed as a function of the log of the scale variable, the log of the user cost of that asset, and the log of the real brokerage fee. The two models differ only in the numerical values predicted for the elasticities and in the nature of the scale variable, which is income for the Baumol-Tobin model and the variance of the unpredictable component of the daily cash flow in the Miller-Orr formulation. In empirical work, values of the elasticities are treated as parameters to be estimated. Hence, a consensus set of inventory theoretic monetary asset demand equations takes the form[22]

$$\ln q_{it} = \alpha_{i0} + \alpha_{i1} \ln Y_t + \alpha_{i2} \ln p_{it} + \alpha_{i3} \ln b_{it} + \varepsilon_t \qquad i = 1, \ldots, N \tag{3.14}$$

Furthermore, as we have seen, the brokerage fee term is usually ignored in empirical work because relevant data are not available.[23]

Now consider the problem of deriving a demand equation for an aggregate of the q_i components, each of which is determined by an equation like 3.14. An equation for the divisia aggregate based on this system is easy to manipulate and to interpret. The divisia monetary quantity aggregate is obtained from the left-hand side of the equation 3.14 by taking the expenditure share-weighted average of first-differences. Doing the same operations to the right-hand side yields

$$\begin{aligned}\sum_i w_{it}^*(\ln q_{it} - \ln q_{i,t-1}) = \sum_i w_{it}^*\alpha_{i0} &+ \sum_i w_{it}^*\alpha_{i1}(\ln Y_t - \ln Y_{t-1}) \\ &+ \sum_i w_{it}^*\alpha_{i2}(\ln p_{it} - \ln p_{i,t-1}) \\ &+ \sum_i w_{it}^*\alpha_{i3}(\ln b_{it} - \ln b_{i,t-1}) \\ &+ \sum_i w_{it}^*\varepsilon_{it}\end{aligned} \tag{3.15}$$

Now assume that it is possible to represent the elasticities of the user cost and brokerage fee terms as follows:

$$\alpha_{i2} = \bar{\alpha}_2 + \eta_i \tag{3.16}$$

$$\alpha_{i3} = \bar{\alpha}_3 + \delta_i \tag{3.17}$$

where η_i and δ_i are components of their respective elasticities that are specific to the ith monetary asset. By construction of $\bar{\alpha}_2$ and $\bar{\alpha}_3$, the means of η_i and δ_i equal zero. Finally, if we assume that the terms in η_i and δ_i can be ignored[24] when the expressions for α_{i2} and α_{i3} are substituted into equation 3.15, then equation 3.15 can be written[25]

$$\begin{aligned}\Sigma w_{it}^*(\ln q_{it} - \ln q_{i,t-1}) = {} & \Sigma w_{it}^*\alpha_{i0} + \Sigma w_{it}^*\alpha_{i1}(\ln Y_t - \ln Y_{t-1}) \\ & + \bar{\alpha}_2 \Sigma w_{it}^*(\ln p_{it} - \ln p_{i,t-1}) \\ & + \bar{\alpha}_3 \Sigma w_{it}^*(\ln b_{it} - \ln b_{i,t-1}) + \Sigma w_{it}^*\varepsilon_{it}\end{aligned} \tag{3.18}$$

But, equation 3.18 is equivalent to

$$\begin{aligned}\ln Q_t - \ln Q_{t-1} = {} & \bar{\alpha}_0 + \bar{\alpha}_1(\ln Y_t - \ln Y_{t-1}) + \bar{\alpha}_2(\ln P_t - \ln P_{t-1}) \\ & + \bar{\alpha}_3(\ln B_t - \ln B_{t-1}) + \bar{\varepsilon}_t\end{aligned} \tag{3.19}$$

where Q_t = the divisia monetary quantity index for assets $i = 1, \ldots, N$
P_t = the divisia monetary user cost index for assets $i = 1, \ldots, N$
B_t = the divisia brokerage fee index for assets $i = 1, \ldots, N$
$\bar{\alpha}_0 = \Sigma\, w_{it}^*\alpha_{i0}$
$\bar{\alpha}_1 = \Sigma\, w_{it}^*\alpha_{i1}$
$\bar{\varepsilon}_t = \Sigma\, w_{it}^*\varepsilon_{it}$

By contrast, the conventional sum aggregate for the system generated by equation 3.14 is extremely cumbersome because adding each side of the set of equations gives a right-hand side which turns out to be a sum of products with parameters as exponents.[26] Thus, divisia aggregation yields a more tractable transactions demand equation than conventional, simple sum aggregation.

Empirical Work

Models. The empirical results reported below are based on two alternative specifications of money demand. The first is a standard double-logarithmic equation similar to the type employed by Goldfeld (1973, 1976) and Bennett et al. (1980). The functional form of this equation is

$$\ln \frac{M_t}{P_t} = \alpha_0 + \alpha_1 \ln Y_t + \alpha_2 \ln R_t + \alpha_3 \ln RPASS_t + \lambda \ln \frac{M_{t-1}}{P_t} + \varepsilon_t \tag{3.20}$$

where R_t = opportunity cost variable, either the three-month Treasury bill rate (RTB) or divisia user cost index, and RPASS denotes the rate paid on passbook savings accounts at commercial banks. The properties of this equation have been discussed elsewhere at length. The second money demand specification is the Porter-Simpson equation first reported in Simpson and Porter (1980) and discussed earlier.

Each of the two specifications is estimated for a number of alternative monetary aggregates and the two alternative opportunity cost variables. The alternative aggregates include conventional sum aggregates and divisia monetary quantity aggregates for eleven sets of components:

1. components of M1 (M1)
2. M1 + overnight RPs + overnight Eurodollars (M1 + Overnights)
3. M1 + noninstitutional money market mutual fund shares (M1 + MMMF2)
4. M1 + Overnights + MMMF2
5. M1 + all money market mutual fund shares (M1 + MMMF3)
6. M1 + Overnights + MMMF3
7. A broad transactions aggregate consisting of components of M1 + Overnights + MMMF3 + large time deposits + bankers' acceptances + commercial paper + short-term Treasury securities + term RPs + term Eurodollars (BROAD TRANS)
8. BROAD TRANS + savings accounts (BROAD TRANS + SAV)
9. components of M2
10. components of M3
11. components of L

The various aggregates and specifications are compared on the basis of three criteria: (1) predictive performance; (2) parameter stability; and (3) consistency of parameter estimates with theoretical considerations. In order to assess predictive performance, each equation is estimated through 1974:2 with the sample period starting in 1959:1 for the double-log equations and in 1955:1 for the Porter-Simpson equation. A dynamic simulation is run for each equation over the period 1974:3–1982:2 with the accuracy of the forecasts being assessed on the basis of traditional forecast error summary statistics. Parameter stability is tested using the familiar Chow test with the break in the respective samples assumed to have occurred after 1974:2. The main issue regarding the consistency of parameter estimates is the size of the estimated coefficient on the lagged dependent variable. Fairly large values of this parameter imply that individuals adjust their actual cash balances toward their long-run desired balances at an extremely slow rate—a finding which we indicated earlier we find implausible for the narrow aggregates. For the broader aggregates, our priors on the value of the lagged dependent variable are not as clear. Nonetheless, it seems reasonable that lagged dependent variables in excess of .8 are implausible inasmuch as such values imply a slow mean adjustment lag of *at least* five quarters. Unfortunately, by this standard most of the empirical results reported are implausible.

Results. Tables 3–6 through 3–15 report selected results from the econometric work just described. The reported findings contain the information relevant for the points that are discussed with the remaining results available on request. Unlike the estimates and simulations discussed in the second section, no adjustments for NOW accounts or other new deposit categories were made in the tables presented.

Tables 3–6 and 3–7 contain results from the Porter-Simpson specification with conventional sum aggregates as the monetary aggregate and the Treasury bill rate as the opportunity cost variable. This set of results can serve as a standard for comparison as it contains results that have been discussed widely in the recent literature. This specification provides the best results for the two narrowest aggregates considered here, M1 and M1 + overnights. In particular, conventional sum aggregation outperforms divisia aggregation at this aggregation level. The mean prediction error statistics are very impressive, and the root mean square errors, while not as good, are among the best obtained for these aggregates. Similarly, while the Chow test F-statistics indicate rejection of parameter stability at the 5 percent level of significance, this specification does have the best F-statistic values for these levels of conventional aggregates. It is also worth noting that when M1 is replaced with an M1-like measure that adjusts for the estimated shifts from savings deposits into NOW accounts, the predictive performance of this specification improved slightly. All in all, it seems reasonable to conclude that sum aggregation and the Porter-Simpson specification provide the most useful formulation for money demand at the very narrowest levels of aggregation.

This conclusion changes drastically when somewhat broader aggregates are considered. In particular, the divisia aggregate for the broad transactions monetary measure provides the best overall results of any aggregate and any

Table 3-6. Error Summary—Porter-Simpson Money Demand Equations: Conventional Aggregates[a] (error statistics for percent growth at annual rates)

Aggregate	*Quarterly Mean Error*	*Quarterly RMSE*	*Annual Mean Error*	*Annual RMSE*	*Chow F-Statistic*[b]
M1	.1	4.0	.3	1.8	2.9
M1 + OVERNIGHTS	−.4	5.3	−.1	1.7	2.8
M1 + MMMF2	−4.0	8.7	−4.1	8.3	7.2
M1 + OVERNIGHTS + MMMF2	−4.1	8.8	−4.3	7.6	5.7
M1 + MMMF3	−4.5	9.6	−4.9	9.4	8.0
M1 + OVERNIGHTS + MMMF3	−4.7	9.5	−5.0	8.7	6.3
BROAD TRANS	−1.4	5.8	−1.0	3.3	.6
BROAD TRANS + SAV	−.8	14.5	.6	3.7	.3
M2	−1.7	3.8	−1.7	2.5	1.8
M3	−1.0	3.5	−1.3	3.0	1.4
L	−1.3	2.7	−1.1	1.7	1.0
MONETARY BASE	2.7	4.7	3.1	4.2	3.3
CURRENCY	.6	2.9	.9	2.3	2.7

[a]Estimation period: 1955:1–1974:2. Simulation period: 1974:3–1982:2. Error = Predicted minus actual.

[b]Degrees of Freedom: 12,88. The hypothesis that the coefficients are equal over the 1955:1–1974:2 and 1974:3–1982:2 sample periods is rejected at the 5% significance level if F is greater than 1.88.

Table 3-7. Annual Errors of Porter-Simpson Money Demand Equations: Conventional Aggregates[a] (percent growth)

Aggregate	*1975*	*1976*	*1977*	*1978*	*1979*	*1980*	*1981*
M1	3.4	1.8	.9	.5	−1.5	−1.1	−1.9
M1 + OVERNIGHTS	3.4	.5	−.4	.1	−1.8	−1.9	−1.0
M1 + MMMF2	2.9	2.0	1.0	−.5	−8.1	−7.7	−18.5
M1 + OVERNIGHTS + MMMF2	2.9	.7	−.3	−.9	−8.1	−8.0	−16.4
M1 + MMMF3	2.8	1.9	.9	−1.1	−9.4	−8.6	−21.0
M1 + OVERNIGHTS + MMMF3	2.9	.6	−.3	−1.4	−9.2	−8.8	−18.8
BROAD TRANS	2.3	4.3	−2.1	−3.6	−5.5	.0	−2.2
BROAD TRANS + SAV	−2.3	5.4	4.0	3.7	1.2	−5.0	−2.5
M2	−1.8	−1.8	−.0	1.4	−2.7	−3.0	−4.2
M3	2.4	2.0	−.3	−1.6	−2.9	−2.3	−6.2
L	−1.1	.5	−.5	−.2	−2.9	−.9	−2.9
MONETARY BASE	4.2	1.3	1.2	.8	.1	5.6	8.6
CURRENCY	−.9	−1.4	−.0	1.3	.4	1.6	5.4

[a]Estimation period: 1955:1–1974:2. Error = Predicted minus actual fourth quarter to fourth quarter growth rates.

specification. The specification providing these results is a standard double-logarithmic equation using the divisia monetary user cost index as the opportunity cost variable. In general, for levels of aggregation that include only assets with some broadly defined transactions property but exclude savings accounts, small time deposits, and U.S. savings bonds, divisia aggregation works better than conventional aggregation.

A brief discussion of some specific results illustrates these points. Tables 3–8 to 3–11 contain results from a standard double-logarithmic specification for divisia aggregates using divisia user costs. Tables 3–12 to 3–15 contain analogous results for conventional sum aggregates. A comparison across aggregates in each pair of corresponding tables reveals that the broad transactions divisia aggregate yields the best overall results. The summary statistics of predictive ability suggest that this divisia aggregate can be predicted about as well as any other. Its Chow test F-statistic value of 1.1 indicates that the stability hypothesis cannot be rejected at the 1 percent significance level and the value of λ in the double-logarithmic equation is an acceptable 0.76 in the early period. These empirical results are not affected materially when the divisia monetary user cost index is replaced by the Treasury bill rate. While the divisia user cost index has greater appeal in terms of consistency with the theory, the Treasury bill rate may have the practical advantage of being forecasted more easily and more accurately. In comparison, the value of λ for the corresponding equation for the conventional sum counterpart is 0.88 in the early period, stability is rejected at the 1 percent level and the error summary statistics are worse.

Similar results are obtained for a somewhat narrower divisia aggregate that includes the components of M1, all money market mutual funds and overnights (M1 + overnights + MMMFs). For this level of aggregation, the divisia aggregate works far better than the sum aggregates in terms of stability and predictive ability. Over the entire period the value of λ equals 0.93 for the divisia aggregate and an inadmissible value of 1.06 for the sum aggregate. The Porter-Simpson equations for these two broader levels of aggregation confirm the contention that divisia aggregation is better than sum aggregation at these aggregation levels.

The Relationship of Divisia Aggregation to the Inventory Approach

The two parts of this paper are based on two approaches to analyzing the well-known problems of money demand that, at first glance, appear to be nearly or totally unrelated. The brokerage fee approach is concerned primarily with explaining the shortfall in demand for one specific monetary asset (demand deposits), and the explanation is based on an omitted variable argument. The divisia monetary aggregates approach is concerned with the entire spectrum of monetary assets, and it relies on an entirely different kind of misspecification argument—incorrect aggregation procedures—to motivate its approach. While these differences are, in fact, quite important, they stem not from fundamental differences about the nature of the monetary mechanism, but rather from alternative approaches in dealing with the limitations in available data. The upshot is that in the absence of these limitations, the two approaches would be entirely complementary, being associated aggregator and index number functions.

The common themes in the two approaches can be expressed by the following unifying model. The brokerage fee approach is based on the traditional inventory-theoretic approach to money demand. In a multiasset framework, the inventory-theoretic approach yields a double-logarithmic system of demand equations for the various monetary assets. In a typical equation, real balances of a given asset are determined as a function of three explanatory variables: (1) a scale variable such as income or the variance of the cash flow; (2) an inventory holding cost variable expressed by an interest rate differential, i.e., the difference between the return on the nonmonetary buffer asset and the own rate on the given monetary asset; and (3) a brokerage fee expressing the cost of converting the given asset into cash. The specification of these equations is somewhat restrictive in that the holding costs and brokerage fees of other assets do not appear in the equation for each given asset. Of course, if the system provides a good empirical formulation for money demand, i.e., if the equations fit well and predict well, then the restrictions are desirable in that they are drawn from sound theory and are not significantly inconsistent with the data. On the other hand, if relevant hypothesis testing suggests that better empirical results might be obtained from a somewhat less restrictive model, then the directions for generalization seem clear. In particular, the inventory-theoretic demand equations are derived from a cost equation that can easily be written as a very general cost function expressing the cost of obtaining a given level of monetary services as a function of interest differentials, brokerage fees, and, possibly, the given value of a scale variable or values of some other relevant variables.

The basis for writing down such a general cost function is the view that individual economic agents face a transactions constraint in addition to the familiar budget constraint and, perhaps, a time constraint. The transactions constraint arises from the need to engage in costly transactions in order to obtain the goods or factors that ultimately yield utility or profit. The use of

Table 3-8. Coefficients of Double-Logarithmic Money Demand Equations: Divisia Aggregates and Divisia User Costs (1959:3 to 1974:2)

	Independent Variables					Summary Statistics			
Aggregate	*Constant*	*Lagged Dependent*	*Divisia User Cost*	*Passbook Rate*	*Real GNP*	$\bar{R}^2$	*Standard Error of Estimate*	ρ	*Durbin-Watson*
M1	−1.118 (−3.18)	.725 (6.65)	−.011 (−1.12)	−.032 (−1.46)	.190 (3.08)	.9994	.00563	.48 (4.2)	1.65
M1 + OVERNIGHTS	−1.127 (−3.19)	.731 (6.84)	−.010 (−1.47)	−.033 (−1.50)	.192 (3.09)	.9994	.00562	.47 (4.2)	1.67
M1 + MMMF2	−1.118 (−3.18)	.725 (6.64)	−.011 (−1.62)	−.032 (−1.48)	.190 (3.08)	.9994	.00563	.48 (4.2)	1.65
M1 + OVERNIGHTS + MMMF2	−1.127 (−3.19)	.731 (6.84)	−.010 (−1.47)	−.033 (−1.50)	.192 (3.09)	.9994	.00561	.47 (4.2)	1.67

M1 + MMMF3	−1.118 (−3.19)	.725 (6.64)	−.011 (−1.62)	−.032 (−1.46)	.190 (3.08)	.9994	.00563	.48 (4.2)	1.65
M1 + OVERNIGHTS + MMMF3	−1.127 (−3.19)	.731 (6.85)	−.010 (−1.47)	−.033 (−1.50)	.192 (3.09)	.9994	.00561	.47 (4.2)	1.67
BROAD TRANS	−1.272 (−3.82)	.756 (9.08)	−.014 (−2.44)	−.035 (−1.67)	.213 (3.71)	.9994	.00597	.49 (4.4)	1.82
BROAD TRANS + SAV	−.832 (−3.63)	.818 (14.2)	−.021 (−3.70)	−.018 (−1.01)	.142 (3.60)	.9994	.00520	.53 (4.8)	1.77
M2	−.843 (−1.93)	.867 (9.83)	−.011 (−2.04)	−.006 (−.27)	.138 (1.89)	.9996	.00536	.71 (7.8)	1.64
M3	−.848 (−1.81)	.891 (10.9)	−.014 (−2.37)	−.003 (−.12)	.137 (1.77)	.9996	.00562	.71 (9.19)	1.59
L	−.950 (−2.40)	.835 (9.57)	−.011 (−2.33)	−.008 (−.39)	.157 (2.35)	.9997	.00478	.69 (7.3)	1.70

Note: t-ratios are shown in parentheses beneath the estimated coefficients.

Table 3-9. Coefficients of Double-Logarithmic Money Demand Equations: Divisia Aggregates and Divisia User Costs (1959:3 to 1982:2)

	Independent Variables					Summary Statistics			
Aggregate	*Constant*	*Lagged Dependent*	*Divisia User Cost*	*Passbook Rate*	*Real GNP*	$\bar{R}^2$	*Standard Error of Estimate*	ρ	*Durbin-Watson*
M1	−.289 (−2.70)	.979 (29.9)	−.014 (−3.17)	.004 (.27)	.045 (2.38)	.9998	.00626	.26 (2.62)	1.89
M1 + OVERNIGHTS	−.346 (−2.69)	.964 (24.0)	−.014 (−3.16)	8.9×10^{-4} (.07)	.055 (2.41)	.9997	.00674	.21 (2.10)	1.93
M1 + MMMF2	−.374 (−3.07)	.942 (22.6)	−.009 (−2.15)	−.001 (−.09)	.061 (2.85)	.9998	.00615	.29 (2.90)	1.93
M1 + OVERNIGHTS + MMMF2	−.441 (−3.07)	.926 (18.8)	−.009 (−2.03)	−.005 (−.37)	.072 (2.83)	.9998	.00655	−.29 (−1.70)	2.05

M1 + MMMF3	−.392 (−3.23)	.939 (22.0)	−.009 (−2.16)	−.003 (−.210)	.064 (2.94)	.9998	.00615	.28 (2.8)	1.95
M1 + OVERNIGHTS + MMMF3	−.449 (−3.12)	.928 (18.7)	−.009 (−2.07)	−.006 (−.48)	.074 (2.87)	.9998	.00650	.20 (1.9)	1.99
BROAD TRANS	−.887 (−4.5)	.867 (17.5)	−.015 (−3.43)	−.026 (−1.47)	.146 (4.33)	.9998	.00603	.51 (5.7)	1.95
BROAD TRANS + SAV	−.206 (−1.13)	.961 (28.2)	−.015 (−2.26)	.012 (.47)	.033 (1.05)	.9995	.00860	.54 (6.09)	2.14
M2	.029 (.13)	1.02 (27.0)	−.008 (−1.50)	.026 (1.09)	−.008 (−.224)	.9997	.00757	.56 (6.4)	2.02
M3	−.071 (−.307)	1.00 (24.9)	−.011 (−2.13)	.022 (.91)	.008 (.211)	.9998	.00695	.641 (8.01)	2.01
L	−.155 (−.77)	.989 (23.4)	−.009 (−2.1)	.014 (.67)	.023 (.68)	.9998	.00608	.67 (8.6)	2.04

Note: t-ratios are shown in parentheses beneath the estimated coefficients.

Table 3-10. Error Summary—Double-Logarithmic Money Demand Equations: Divisia Aggregates and Divisia User Costs[a] (error statistics for percent growth at annual rates)

Aggregate	*Quarterly Mean Error*	*Quarterly RMSE*	*Annual Mean Error*	*Annual RMSE*	*Chow F-Statistic*[b]
M1	1.5	3.2	1.9	2.1	4.3
M1 + OVERNIGHTS	1.2	3.5	1.6	1.9	5.0
M1 + MMMF2	.4	3.0	.8	1.6	3.6
M1 + OVERNIGHTS + MMMF2	.2	3.3	.5	1.4	3.8
M1 + MMMF3	.3	3.0	.6	1.6	4.1
M1 + OVERNIGHTS + MMMF3	.1	3.2	.3	1.3	4.5
BROAD TRANS	−.6	3.0	−.3	1.8	1.1
BROAD TRANS + SAV	2.9	6.0	3.4	5.2	6.0
M2	2.3	5.7	2.7	5.3	5.1
M3	2.4	5.0	2.8	4.8	2.9
L	2.1	4.7	2.5	4.5	2.9

[a]Estimation period: 1959:3–1974:2. Simulation period: 1974:3–1982:2. Error = Predicted minus actual.

[b]Degrees of Freedom: 5,82. The hypothesis that the coefficients are equal over the 1959:3–1974:2 and the 1974:3–1982:2 sample periods is rejected at the 5% significance level if F is greater than 2.33.

Table 3-11. Annual Errors of Double-Logarithmic Money Demand Equations: Divisia Aggregates and Divisia User Costs[a] (percent growth)

Aggregate	*1975*	*1976*	*1977*	*1978*	*1979*	*1980*	*1981*
M1	2.1	2.2	1.5	2.0	2.2	.0	3.1
M1 + OVERNIGHTS	1.9	1.3	.8	1.8	2.3	−.4	3.3
M1 + MMMF2	2.0	2.3	1.5	1.5	.5	−1.7	−.8
M1 + OVERNIGHTS + MMMF2	1.8	1.5	.8	1.4	.6	−2.0	−.5
M1 + MMMF3	2.0	2.3	1.5	1.3	.2	−1.6	−1.4
M1 + OVERNIGHTS + MMMF3	1.8	1.4	.8	1.1	.3	−1.9	−1.1
BROAD TRANS	1.3	2.9	−1.1	−1.1	.4	−1.9	−2.7
BROAD TRANS + SAV	−1.0	−.4	−.1	4.1	9.8	3.5	8.1
M2	−3.6	−3.1	.4	5.3	8.6	3.4	7.7
M3	−2.1	−1.6	−.0	4.5	8.8	3.2	6.6
L	−2.1	−1.4	−.8	3.4	8.0	3.9	6.7

[a]Estimation period: 1959:3–1974:2. Error = Predicted minus actual fourth quarter to fourth quarter growth rates.

Table 3-12. Coefficients of Double-Logarithmic Money Demand Equations: Conventional Aggregates and Interest Rate Opportunity Costs (1959:3 to 1974:2)

	Independent Variables					Summary Statistics			
Aggregate	*Constant*	*Lagged Dependent*	*RTB*	*Passbook Rate*	*Real GNP*	$\bar{R}^2$	*Standard Error of Estimate*	ρ	*Durbin-Watson*
M1	.447 (1.29)	.757 (7.16)	−.013 (−3.02)	−.016 (−1.10)	.133 (3.45)	.9995	.00442	.45 (3.9)	1.80
M1 + OVERNIGHTS	.468 (1.48)	.720 (6.90)	−.011 (−2.62)	−.023 (−1.65)	.160 (3.85)	.9996	.00430	.42 (3.6)	1.85
M1 + MMMF2	.467 (1.34)	.751 (7.10)	−.013 (−2.99)	−.015 (−1.13)	.135 (3.51)	.9995	.00440	.45 (3.9)	1.80
M1 + OVERNIGHTS + MMMF2	.473 (1.49)	.719 (6.89)	−.011 (−2.50)	−.023 (−1.66)	.161 (3.87)	.9996	.00430	.42 (3.6)	1.85
M1 + MMMF3	.473 (1.36)	.749 (7.09)	−.013 (−2.98)	−.016 (−1.13)	.136 (3.53)	.9995	.00440	.45 (3.9)	1.80

M1 + OVERNIGHTS + MMMF3	.475	.718	−.011	−.023	.161	.9996	.00429	.42	1.85
	(1.50)	(6.88)	(−2.58)	(−1.66)	(3.88)			(3.6)	
BROAD TRANS	−.244	.880	.009	.004	.137	.9994	.00744	.69	2.17
	(−1.18)	(11.9)	(1.04)	(.15)	(2.05)			(7.4)	
BROAD TRANS + SAV	−.050	.933	−.010	.008	.073	.9997	.00485	.75	2.03
	(−.23)	(15.1)	(−1.68)	(.39)	(1.75)			(8.9)	
M2	−.281	.983	−.027	.014	.062	.9999	.00380	.42	1.85
	(−3.66)	(22.2)	(−7.57)	(1.27)	(1.38)			(3.6)	
M3	−.277	.999	−.027	.036	.035	.9998	.00486	.62	1.78
	(−1.50)	(19.0)	(−5.05)	(2.02)	(.54)			(6.1)	
L	−.203	.999	−.014	.019	.033	.9999	.00381	.58	2.04
	(−2.25)	(17.7)	(−3.47)	(1.47)	(.58)			(5.5)	
MONETARY BASE	.075	.752	−.001	−.005	.149	.9996	.00480	.24	1.89
	(.74)	(8.77)	(−.28)	(−.39)	(3.08)			(1.9)	
CURRENCY	−.139	.816	.001	.006	.124	.9999	.00271	.41	2.02
	(−2.62)	(16.5)	(.42)	(.68)	(3.99)			(3.5)	

Note: t-ratios are shown in parentheses beneath the estimated coefficients.

Table 3-13. Coefficients of Double-Logarithmic Money Demand Equations: Conventional Aggregates and Interest Rate Opportunity Costs (1959:3 to 1982:2)

	Independent Variables					*Summary Statistics*			
Aggregate	*Constant*	*Lagged Dependent*	*RTB*	*Passbook Rate*	*Real GNP*	$\bar{R}^2$	*Standard Error of Estimate*	ρ	*Durbin-Watson*
M1	−.263 (−2.48)	1.01 (51.5)	−.010 (−3.36)	-4.6×10^{-4} (−.05)	.035 (3.18)	.9997	.00621	.01 (.1)	1.99
M1 + OVERNIGHTS	−.263 (−1.87)	.994 (30.0)	−.011 (−3.47)	−.006 (−.53)	.048 (3.29)	.9996	.00792	−.14 (−1.4)	2.01
M1 + MMMF2	−.340 (−1.77)	1.01 (28.6)	.001 (.27)	−.013 (−.73)	.044 (2.15)	.9996	.00802	.36 (3.7)	2.12
M1 + OVER-NIGHTS + MMMF2	−.508 (−3.59)	1.06 (36.5)	−.002 (−.32)	−.012 (−.87)	.034 (2.02)	.9996	.00897	.01 (.1)	1.93
M1 + MMMF3	−.449 (−2.40)	1.03 (31.3)	-1.8×10^{-4} (−.03)	−.016 (−.85)	.046 (2.18)	.9996	.00894	.31 (3.1)	2.10

M1 + OVER-NIGHTS + MMMF3	−.554 (−4.06)	1.06 (40.5)	−.003 (−.52)	−.014 (−.96)	.036 (2.10)	.9995	.00953	.01 (.1)	1.91
BROAD TRANS	−.402 (−2.45)	.924 (32.6)	.015 (2.25)	−.026 (−.89)	.127 (3.21)	.9998	.00762	.69 (9.1)	2.13
BROAD TRANS + SAV	−.046 (−.29)	.926 (20.6)	−.009 (−2.00)	.007 (.38)	.079 (2.54)	.9999	.00594	.58 (6.8)	2.15
M2	−.253 (−3.48)	.904 (22.7)	−.023 (−6.72)	.023 (1.90)	.129 (3.14)	.9999	.00467	.43 (4.5)	1.96
M3	−.285 (−2.42)	.930 (23.1)	−.018 (−4.74)	.033 (1.88)	.108 (2.14)	.9999	.00466	.67 (8.6)	1.77
L	−.228 (−3.10)	.949 (29.2)	−.009 (−3.24)	.013 (1.07)	.085 (2.35)	1.000	.00362	.62 (7.6)	1.92
MONETARY BASE	−.170 (−1.79)	1.05 (38.8)	−.001 (−.39)	.011 (.86)	−.005 (−.27)	.9998	.00579	.32 (3.3)	1.96
CURRENCY	−.120 (−2.20)	.922 (20.8)	−.004 (−1.80)	.019 (2.03)	.061 (2.04)	1.000	.00324	.45 (4.9)	2.00

Note: t-ratios are shown in parentheses beneath the estimated coefficients.

Table 3-14. Error Summary—Double-Logarithmic Money Demand Equations: Divisia Aggregates and Divisia User Costs[a] (error statistics for percent growth at annual rates)

Aggregate	*Quarterly Mean Error*	*Quarterly RMSE*	*Annual Mean Error*	*Annual RMSE*	*Chow F-Statistic*[b]
M1	2.0	4.0	2.2	2.8	4.6
M1 + OVERNIGHTS	1.2	5.1	1.4	2.4	6.6
M1 + MMMF2	−2.1	6.4	−2.3	6.1	10.3
M1 + OVERNIGHTS + MMMF2	−2.6	6.8	−2.7	5.6	11.0
M1 + MMMF3	−2.7	7.3	−3.1	7.1	9.2
M1 + OVERNIGHTS + MMMF3	−3.1	7.5	−3.5	6.6	10.3
BROAD TRANS	−2.6	5.4	−3.0	5.3	3.2
BROAD TRANS + SAV	−.4	3.2	−.3	1.5	2.1
M2	−.9	3.2	−.8	2.5	2.5
M3	.8	3.4	1.0	3.2	2.5
L	.4	2.0	.5	1.6	1.4
MONETARY BASE	2.7	3.9	2.9	3.7	4.3
CURRENCY	.5	2.0	.8	1.9	3.8

[a]Estimation period: 1959:3–1974:2. Simulation period: 1974:3–1982:2. Error = Predicted minus actual.

[b]Degrees of Freedom: 5,82. The hypothesis that the coefficients are equal over the 1959:3–1974:2 and the 1974:3–1982:2 sample periods is rejected at the 5% significance level if F is greater than 2.33.

Table 3-15. Annual Errors of Double-Logarithmic Money Demand Equations: Conventional Aggregates and Interest Rate Opportunity Costs[a] (percent growth)

Aggregate	*1975*	*1976*	*1977*	*1978*	*1979*	*1980*	*1981*
M1	5.0	3.2	.7	.5	.7	1.0	4.0
M1 + OVERNIGHTS	4.5	1.4	−.6	.1	.4	.0	4.2
M1 + MMMF2	4.5	3.3	.7	−.5	−5.9	−5.7	−12.6
M1 + OVERNIGHTS + MMMF2	3.9	1.6	−.6	−.8	−5.9	−6.2	−11.3
M1 + MMMF3	4.4	3.2	.7	−1.1	−7.2	−6.5	−15.1
M1 + OVERNIGHTS + MMMF3	3.9	1.5	−.6	−1.4	−7.1	−7.0	−13.7
BROAD TRANS	3.9	2.7	−4.5	−7.1	−6.8	−1.9	−7.5
BROAD TRANS + SAV	2.1	.7	−2.1	−1.6	.5	−.3	−2.0
M2	−1.8	−.3	2.1	2.6	−.8	−2.7	−4.7
M3	3.8	4.4	3.3	1.6	−.1	−1.3	−4.9
L	2.0	2.4	1.0	.2	−1.0	.9	−2.4
MONETARY BASE	4.7	1.9	1.3	−.0	1.0	4.2	6.8
CURRENCY	−.5	−.9	−.2	.5	1.3	.5	4.8

[a]Estimation period: 1959:3–1974:2. Error = Predicted minus actual fourth quarter to fourth quarter growth rates.

monetary assets is desirable in that it allows individuals to conserve time and other resources that would otherwise be required to carry out the desired transactions. If it is assumed that individuals optimize, then it is necessarily the case that individuals hold the amounts of monetary assets that maximize the conservation of other resources for any level of transactions.[27]

An alternative way of expressing the transactions constraint is by writing down a cost function, dual to the transactions constraint, that expresses the minimum holding plus brokerage cost of obtaining a given level of monetary services. One problem with writing down such a cost function is that the brokerage fees are usually assessed on the basis of units that are different from the units that determine an asset's return. The return is nearly always determined by the average balance, while brokerage fees depend either on the number or the volume of transactions. Thus, some degree of averaging is required to arrive at a unique, relevant concept of overall marginal cost. The aggregation methods presented here do not address this problem and, in any event, the lack of direct information on brokerage fees renders this question moot from an empirical standpoint.

In an ideal situation where all relevant data on brokerage fees and returns are available, the inventory-theoretic demand equation system, as well as more general systems, can be estimated directly. Divisia monetary quantity and user cost indexes can also be constructed from the same data that are used to estimate the monetary asset demand equations. In the ideal world with all relevant data, the user costs thus reflect both the return differentials and the brokerage fees. In this situation, the estimated demand equations and the divisia index numbers are complements. The demand equations would be used in traditional econometric roles such as policy evaluation and forecasting. The index numbers are data; some may be used as targets of policy and all may be used as objects of economic analysis. The index numbers serve as proxies for economic concepts that can also be measured using estimated parameters from the demand systems. For example, suppose the transactions constraint can be written as the implicit function $F(y,T,M)$, where y is a vector of goods, T is time saved by using monetary assets in transactions, and $M = f(m,\alpha)$, where m is a vector of monetary asset quantities and α is a parameter vector. Then the elements of α can be derived from the demand equation system's parameters. Hence the function of interest, $f(m,\alpha)$, can be evaluated usually up to a constant using these estimates. However, in many cases, there is considerable controversy regarding the techniques used to obtain estimates of α. In general, it is best to avoid the use of such complicated statistical techniques in generating statistical data series such as money supply numbers. Index number theory allows for the measurement of economic concepts without relying on complex statistical tools. Diewert (1974) has shown that certain index numbers, including the divisia index, approximate the true unknown economic concept, and these index number formulas involve calculations that are considerably less formidable and intuitively more transparent than the calculations that underlie the statistically estimated parameters. Accordingly, the index numbers are useful as published data, while the demand systems are used for deeper analysis.

In the real world of imperfect data, the differences between the index number approach to monetary aggregation and the demand systems approach are more extensive. The lack of hard data on brokerage fees is just one example of the potential problems caused by unobservables. Because the divisia monetary index numbers are intended to serve as raw data for further analysis, these indexes must be generated from highly reputable, well-established underlying sources. The type of rough brokerage fee series presented here are not at all suitable for these indexes. Accordingly, the divisia indexes currently suffer from the deficiency of not incorporating any information on these charges. If deregulation of financial markets proceeds as planned and brokerage fees become more prevalent, it is conceivable that some hard data on these charges will become available on a regular basis. The conceptual basis for incorporating these data in the divisia index numbers should be developed as soon as the prospects for the availability of this data become realistic. Before that, the available divisia indexes should be viewed as approximations to the ideal indexes. The usefulness of the approximation will depend on the performance of the indexes in the applications involving them. The demand equations that involve brokerage fees are also subject to certain difficulties as discussed elsewhere in the paper. For example, the brokerage fee proxy is obtained through a fairly indirect procedure, and only one equation of a multiequation system has been estimated.

Given the problems that affect both approaches, it is possible to ask whether the entire body of work can be viewed fruitfully in a unified perspective. The answer is that the two approaches are attempts to come to grips with the same basic problem—the need to improve our ability to explain and forecast money demand. In an ideal world, the two approaches are complementary concepts derived from a common basis, with the inventory-theoretic approach being a particularly appealing specialization of the more general theory of individual optimization. In trying to make the best of a situation with considerable data limitations, the approaches emphasize different types of information. It is possible that an accumulation of empirical evidence will lead to a consensus rejecting one approach in favor of the other. Until that occurs, both approaches can be analyzed and their implications can be treated as complementary pieces of information in addressing policy questions. When the implications differ, an investigation of the sources of difference may prove insightful.

Notes

1. See the third section for a demonstration of this assertion.

2. Prior to 1981, the adjusted series is constructed as an estimate of what M1-A would have been if four deposit categories—ATS accounts nationwide, NOW accounts in the Northeast, and savings accounts for businesses and for state and local govenments—had not been permitted. See Lindsey et al. (1981, table 10, footnote 2) for further details. For 1981 the growth rate of shift-adjusted M1-B is used to generate the adjusted series. See also Parke and Taubman (1982) for cross-section regression evidence covering 9,000 banks indicating the statistical foundations for the 1981 shift adjustment. The second section employs shift adjustments since the focus is on demand deposits. The third section, which considers a broad range of aggregates, does not use any adjustments.

3. See John Judd and John Scadding (1982) for a survey of this research.

4. See Simpson and Porter (1980), appendix A, part III for a detailed discussion of several cash management techniques.

5. In Simpson and Porter (1980), three alternative functional forms were used. In subsequent work, the product form of the ratchet variable has been used exclusively.

6. The ratchet variable is defined as the cumulative sum of the positive elements of the difference between the current five-year rate on U.S. government notes and a 12-quarter moving average of recent yields on these securities.

7. In this regard, it is interesting that Swamy, Tinsley, and Moore (1982) find that in a general stochastic coefficients framework, the intercept (omitted variables) explain a greater proportion of real balances than any other explanatory variable in the standard money demand specification.

8. In the Miller-Orr (1966) model (see Orr, 1969, pp. 55–62), expected financial transactions may be determined as follows. Recall that in the model, cash balances follow a Bernoulli process with probability equal to 1/2; they fluctuate between a ceiling balance and a floor balance of zero. Whenever these limits are reached, the cash balance is restored to an intermediate level, the return point. In the Orr's derivation of the properties of the rule, he assumes that each *nonfinancial* transaction is in units of m dollars and that there are t transactions per day. Thus, the cash balances fluctuate between a floor of zero and a ceiling of hm, each fluctuation within the bounds being m dollars at a time. He then makes a change of variable so that the standard cash unit is m dollars rather than one dollar. If z is the return point for the cash balance, the probability of reaching the ceiling h and debiting the deposit account is

$$\text{Prob} = \frac{t}{2} \; \frac{2}{h(h-z)}$$

(see Orr, 1969, pp. 60–61). Thus, expected financial debits, Ed, are

$$\text{Ed} = \text{Prob} \cdot (h - z)$$

since a transfer of $h - z$ is made whenever the upper boundary is reached. But at the optimum $h = 3z$ so that

$$\mathrm{Ed} = \frac{t}{3z}$$

To convert from units of m dollars to dollars, Ed must be multiplied by m; i.e., expected debits in dollars (ED) is

$$\mathrm{ED} = \frac{\mathrm{mt}}{3z}$$

But at the optimum, Orr shows that the return point z is on average related to the underlying determinants according to

$$z = \left(\frac{3bt}{4rm}\right)^{1/3}$$

where r and b denote the interest and brokerage fee, respectively. Thus

$$(3\mathrm{ED})^3 = \frac{m^3t^3}{\dfrac{3bt}{4rm}} = \frac{m^4t^2t}{3b} = \frac{y^4r}{3b}$$

where y, the standard deviation of the daily cash flow, equals m^2t—corresponding to t transactions daily each with variance m^2. Thus

$$\mathrm{ED} = \alpha_{2h}\left(\frac{ry^4}{b}\right)^{1/3}$$

where

$$\alpha_{2h} = \frac{1}{3}\left(\frac{1}{3}\right)^{1/3}$$

The expression for ED is the debits equation 3.3 quoted in the text.

9. Recent developments in automatic teller machines (ATM) provide an interesting example of how such a correlation might arise. The increased availability of ATMs should increase money changing transactions from transaction accounts to currency. However, as more and more ATMs are linked together in regional (or national) computer networks, the costs of other types of transactions, including electronic funds transfer, should also fall leading to a more general reduction in brokerage fees. For a survey of the impact of ATMs on electronic banking networks, see "Electronic Banking," *Business Week*, January 18, 1982, pp. 70–80.

10. There is an inherent inconsistency in the sense that $b^{(t)}$ is defined in terms of theoretical parameter estimates whereas equation 3.5 is viewed as the *usual* empirical money demand function which is assumed to obey only sign restrictions on the parameters.

11. Essentially we only deviated from his method to avoid double counting of a construction series.

12. For the GNP deflator, only the seasonally adjusted series is available. Presumably, the seasonality in the deflator is relatively minor compared with the seasonality in nominal GNP. On the other hand, the brokerage series variable can be obtained on both a not seasonally adjusted and seasonally adjusted basis. The role of the brokerage fee as the missing variable in the money demand function lies in its secular, not its seasonal movements. Thus, *seasonally adjusted* GNP and financial debits are used to obtain $b^{(t)}$. The equation incorporates the treasury bill rate as the interest rate measure in the definition of $b^{(t)}$.

13. We are indebted to Marvin Goodfriend (1982b) for making this point. He considers the problem under the following assumptions: suppose there is no lag between money holdings and income in the true structural relationship

$$m_t = a_0 + a_1 y_t + e_t$$

where y_t = the true scale variable in the money demand function

e_t = true disturbance in this structural equation.

However, the actual scale variable used in the empirical regression is measured with error

$$y_t^m = y_t + \zeta_t$$

where ζ_t is the random white noise measurement error in the estimate of y_t which has variance σ_ζ^2. Suppose also that the process generating the true scale variable y_t is a first-order autoregressive process

$$y_t = \phi_0 + \phi_1 y_{t-1} + u_t$$

where u_t is also a white noise process. Now assume that the analyst estimates a "conventional" demand equation

$$\eta_t = b_0 + b_1 y_t^m + b_2 m_{t-1} + v_t$$

The properties of the least-squares estimates of (b_2) the lagged dependent variables are

$$\text{plim}\, b_2 = \frac{\sigma_\xi^2 a_1^2 \phi_1 \sigma_u^2/(1 - \phi_1^2)}{\dfrac{\sigma_\zeta^2(a_1^2\sigma^2 u + \sigma_e^2)}{1 - \phi_1^2} + \dfrac{(a_1^2\sigma_u^2 + \sigma_e^2)\sigma_u^2}{1 - \phi_1^2}}$$

Thus, if measurement error exists, that is, $\sigma_\zeta^2 > 0$, then plim $b_2 > 0$ if $\phi_1 > 0$. Also it can be immediately verified that

$$\frac{\partial\, \text{plimb}_2}{\partial \sigma_\zeta^2} > 0$$

Thus, an increase in the variance of the measurement error, other things equal, will lead to an increase in the estimated lagged dependent variable.

14. All variables had the correct sign and were significant in these DDOS regressions.

15. The argument does not apply directly to the DDOS nonfinancial business deposits data. It may be also noted that the Board's series on turnover was based on a different deposit concept than the money supply until the 1977 revision. Finally, the statistical results do not appear to be consistent with the notion that the results are merely circular.

16. The matrix of regressors corresponding to equation 3.7 is a linear transformation, the matrix of regressors corresponding to equation 3.8. Since the transformation is linear and nonsingular, the projections must be equivalent. For the results to be identical, not seasonally adjusted GNP must be used to obtain $b^{(d)}$ (see footnote 12 above); the results are not much affected by using seasonally adjusted GNP instead but the equivalence does not hold exactly in this case.

It should also be noted that the lagged dependent variables in the regressions are also implausibly large.

17. In any event, data are not available to separate nonstore of weath services into monetary and other services, but this is probably because there are almost no nonmonetary, nonstore of wealth services.

18. This result is strictly correct only in continuous time. A formal treatment yielding this result is in Fisher and McAleer (1979). In discrete time, the interest differential must be discounted to the beginning of the period. Barnett (1980) has derived the formula rigorously in an analysis that also treats taxation. Taxes are ignored here because a time series on the average marginal tax rate is not available.

Note that the relevant opportunity cost is the foregone interest rather than the price of obtaining one unit (one dollar) of the asset because we are concerned with a finite holding period after which individuals reevaluate their decision regarding how much of each asset to hold.

19. See, for example, Offenbacher (1982a).

20. Economic index numbers come in price and quantity pairs. A desirable property of an index number, known as a factor reversal, states that the product of the price and quantity indexes should be equal the expenditure index. In the present application, the quantity index is obtained by direct calculation of the divisia index formula; the price index is obtained from factor reversal by dividing the expenditure index by the quantity index.

21. Strictly, the divisia index is defined in continuous time. The formula in the text is the Tornquist-Theil discrete time approximation to the divisia index.

22. In this section, upper case letters denote aggregate variables and lower case variables denote components of the aggregates.

23. The second section, of course, is an exception to this general rule.

24. A better treatment of the aggregation problem would treat the terms in η_i and δ_i as part of the disturbance in each equation. The assumptions needed to arrive at equation 3.14 can then be derived explicitly. It should be obvious that, although these assumptions are not innocuous, they are far less restrictive and complicated than the assumptions that would be needed to get simple equations for conventional sum aggregates. For treatments of this sort dealing with aggregation over individual economic agents, see Theil (1971), pp. 570 ff, and Barnett (1979).

25. If the same set of steps is carried out, except for first differencing, the indexes obtained are of the form $\Sigma w_{it} \ln x_{it}$, where x represents a quantity, a user cost, or a brokerage fee. This index is cited by Deaton and Muellbauer (1980) as Stone's index.

26. Of course the growth rate of a conventional sum aggregate is also a weighted sum of the component growth rates so a similar exercise could be carried out for these aggregates. The weights in the sum aggregate case assume that all user costs are equal. The problem with such an exercise is that the resulting right-hand side indexes are difficult to interpret, having no basis in index number theory or other economic theory.

27. For example, seasonal dummies, a trend, or a proxy for cash management services. An

example of a demand system for monetary assets that includes such predetermined variables is in Offenbacher (1982b).

28. There is an implicit assumption that the monetary assets constitute a homothetically separable block in the transactions technology.

References

Barnett, William A. "The User Cost of Money." *Economics Letters* (Vol. 1, 1978), 145–49.

Barnett, William A. "Theoretical Foundations for the Rotterdam Model." *Review of Economic Studies* (Vol. 46, 1979), 109–130.

Barnett, William A. "Economic Monetary Aggregation: An Application of Index Number and Aggregation Theory." *Journal of Econometrics* (September 1980), 11–48.

Barnett, William A. *Consumer Demand and Labor Supply: Goods, Monetary Assets and Time*. Amsterdam: North-Holland, 1980.

Barnett, William A. "New Indices of Money Supply and the Flexible Laurent Demand System." *Journal of Economic and Business Statistics* (January 1983).

Barnett, William A. and Paul A. Spindt. "Divisia Monetary Aggregates: Compilation, Data and Historical Behavior," Staff Economic Studies 116. Washington, D. C.: Board of Governors of the Federal Reserve System, 1982.

Barnett, William A., Paul A. Spindt, and Edward K. Offenbacher. "Empirical Comparisons of Divisia and Simple Sum Monetary Aggregates." Conference Paper 122, National Bureau of Economic Research, 1981.

Bennett, David, Flint Brayton, Eileen Mauskopf, Edward K. Offenbacher, and Richard Porter. "Econometric Properties of the Newly Defined Monetary Aggregates." Washington, D.C.: Board of Governors of the Federal Reserve System, Division of Research and Statistics, processed, February 1980.

Cramer, J. S. "The Regular and Irregular Circulation of Money." Paper presented at the 1980 Meetings of the American Economic Association. University of Amsterdam, Faculty of Actuarial Science and Econometrics, 1980.

Deaton, Angus S. and John Muellbauer. "An Almost Ideal Demand System." *American Economic Review* (June 1980), 312–326.

Diewert, W. E. "Exact and Superlative Index Numbers." *Journal of Econometrics* (Vol. 4, 1978), 115–146.

Enzler, Jared, Lewis Johnson, and John Paulus. "Some Problems of Money Demand." *Brookings Papers on Economic Activity* (1976:1), 261–280.

Farr, Helen T., Richard D. Porter, and Eleanor M. Pruitt. "Demand Deposit Ownership Survey." In *Improving the Monetary Aggregates: Staff Papers*. Washington, D.C.: Board of Governors of the Federal Reserve System, pp. 91–116.

Fisher, Gordon, and Michael McAleer. "Theory and Econometric Evaluation of a

Systems Approach to the Demand for Money: The Canadian Case." Queen's University Department of Economics Working Paper No. 367. 1979

Goldberger, A. S. "Maximum Likelihood Estimation of Regressions Containing Unobservable Independent Variables." *International Economic Review* (Vol. 13, 1972), 1–14.

Goldfeld, Steven. "The Demand for Money Revisited." *Brookings Papers on Economic Activity* (1973:3), 577–638.

Goldfeld, Steven. "The Case of the Missing Money." *Brookings Papers on Economic Activity* (1976:3), 683–730.

Goodfriend, Marvin. "Transaction Cost, Dynamics and the Specification and Estimation of Money Demand." Unpublished paper, 1982a.

Goodfriend, Marvin. "Measurement Error and a Reinterpretation of the Conventional Money Demand Function." Unpublished paper, 1982b.

Judd, John P. and John L. Scadding. "The Search for a Stable Money Demand Function: A Survey of the Post–1973 Literature." *Journal of Economic Literature* (September 1982), 993–1023.

Lieberman, Charles. "The Transactions Demand for Money and Technological Change," *Review of Economics and Statistics* (August 1977), 307–317.

Lindsey, David, Helen Farr, Gary Gillum, Kenneth Kopecky, Eileen Mauskopf, Edward Offenbacher, Richard Porter, John Judd, John Scadding, and Albert Berger. "Monetary Control Experience Under the New Operating Procedures." *New Monetary Control Procedures*, Vol. II. Washington, D.C.: Board of Governors of the Federal Reserve System, 1981.

Mauskopf, Eileen and Richard D. Porter. "Cash Management and the Mid-Seventies Shift in the Demand for Demand Deposits in the U.S." Forthcoming in *Proceedings of Rome Conference on Monetary and Financial Models*. (Editions ECONOMICA, Paris, 1979).

Miller, Merton and Daniel Orr. "A Model of the Demand for Money by Firms." *Quarterly Journal of Economics* (Vol. 80, 1966), 413–435.

Offenbacher, Edward. "The Substitutability of Monetary Assets." Ph.D. dissertation, University of Chicago, 1979.

Offenbacher, Edward. "Questions and Answers on Divisia Monetary Aggregates." (Washington, D.C.: Board of Governors of the Federal Reserve System, Division of Research and Statistics, processed, 1982a.

Offenbacher, Edward. "The Effects of Substitution Among Assets and Technological Innovation on Money Demand." *1982 Proceedings of the Business and Economics Section of the American Statistical Association*, forthcoming.

Offenbacher, Edward and Richard D. Porter. "Update and Extensions on Econometric Properties of Money Demand." Washington, D.C.: Board of Governors of the Federal Reserve System, Division of Research and Statistics, processed, 1982.

Orr, Daniel. *Cash Management and the Demand for Money*. New York: Praeger, 1969.

Parke, Darrel and Stephan B. Taubman. "Cross-Section Regression Estimates of the

Sources of NOW Account Deposits." *1982 Proceedings of the Business and Economics Section of the American Statistical Association*, forthcoming.

Porter, Richard D. "Debits, Turnover and Money Demand." Washington, D.C.: Board of Governors of the Federal Reserve System, Division of Research and Statistics, processed, 1976.

Porter, Richard D., Thomas D. Simpson, and Eileen Mauskopf. "Financial Innovation and the Monetary Aggregates." *Brookings Papers on Economic Activity* (1979:1), 213–29.

Quick, Perry D. and John Paulus. "Financial Innovations and the Transactions Demand for Money." Washington, D.C.: Board of Governors of the Federal Reserve System, Division of Research and Statistics, Banking Section, processed, 1979.

Simpson, Thomas D. "The Market for Federal Funds and Repurchase Agreements." Staff Studies 106, Board of Governors of the Federal Reserve System, July 1979.

Simpson, Thomas D. and Richard D. Porter. "Some Issues Involving the Definition and Interpretation of the Monetary Aggregates." In *Controlling Monetary Aggregates III*. Federal Reserve Bank of Boston Conference Series No. 22, 1980.

Swamy, P. A. V. B., Peter A. Tinsley, and George R. Moore. "An Autopsy of a Conventional Macroeconomic Relation: The Case of Money Demand." Washington, D.C.: Board of Governors of the Federal Reserve System, Division of Research and Statistics, Special Studies Section, processed, 1982.

Theil, Henri. *Principles of Econometrics*. New York: John Wiley and Sons.

DISCUSSION

Scott E. Hein

The Porter-Offenbacher paper provides extensive evidence in support of two propositions. The first proposition is that the quantity of narrow money demanded was lowered in the mid-1970s by technological innovations that improved cash management capabilities. This proposition suggests that money demand did not shift exogenously at that time, as many have suggested. Rather, there was an endogenous movement in real balances as a result of these innovations. The second proposition supported by Porter and Offenbacher is that the demand for monetary aggregates broader than M1 is better understood when these aggregates are measured using a weighted-sum aggregation procedure, rather than the conventional simple-sum method.

I will focus primarily on the first proposition in my comments. But first, I would like to address a broader issue. Accepting these propositions as true, we are still left with the important question, "So what?" Specifically, for a conference of this type, the natural questions that should be asked are: How does this knowledge relate to monetary policy? and Does this information suggest ways of improving monetary policy?

I'm sorry to say that the Porter-Offenbacher paper offers little aid in understanding the policy implications of their findings. I think this shortcoming is very serious since their analysis does raise important policy issues.

The most obvious question they fail to come to grips with is which monetary aggregate represents the best target. Their paper clearly broaches the issue of *the* measurement of money (witness the title of their paper, "Financial Innovations and *the* Measurement of *the* Money Supply" [emphasis added]). I would argue the Federal Reserve effectively has only one tool—the adjusted monetary base. With only one tool, the Federal Reserve only can affect one target. Which target is preferable, then? Porter and Offenbacher never directly address this issue, although their framework supposedly has much to say about the relationship between a monetary aggregate (target) and economic activity. In large part, we are left in the dark as to what to make of their findings.

Narrower Money and the Brokerage Fee

Rather than delving into the meaning of their findings, Porter and Offenbacher spend their time developing evidence in support of their two propositions. Thus, to be fair, I should spend my time evaluating that evidence. Porter and Offenbacher investigate whether improvements in cash management techniques have caused real M1 balances to deviate from levels predicted by conventional demand models. The difficulty in testing this hypothesis is quantifying the improvements in cash management techniques that have supposedly taken place.

Porter and Simpson, at an earlier Boston Federal Reserve conference, proxied such improvements by a ratchet variable that rose as interest rates reached new peaks—the argument being that when interest rates rise to new peak levels, firms are led to undertake new fixed investment in cash management procedures, thus lowering desired cash balances.

The present paper proposes an alternative proxy for such effects. As such, it must be interpreted as an admission that the Porter-Simpson money demand specification is not fully satisfactory. I say this not to castigate Dick Porter, but rather as a contrasting evaluation to David Lindsey, who, at last year's conference, highly praised the Porter-Simpson equation.

In the present paper, Porter and Offenbacher raise the possibility that the improvements in cash management procedures may not be induced solely by rising interest rates, but rather may have originated in exogenous technological innovations—for example, an invention that improves computer technology. The Porter-Simpson variable would not capture the latter effect, so Porter and Offenbacher now propose an alternative methodology that would capture both induced and exogenous cash management improvements. They argue that what is missing in a conventional money demand equation is a brokerage fee—measuring the cost of transferring money into other financial assets and vice versa. This brokerage fee supposedly was lowered in the mid-1970s either because firms invested more in cash management or because of technological breakthroughs.

On a theoretical level, they are quite right in calling attention to the brokerage fee. The inventory theoretic foundations of Baumol (1952) and Tobin (1956), for example, clearly recognize the importance of such a variable. Thus, this hypothesis appears worthy of our attention.

Past empirical work usually has ignored the brokerage fee variable, however, because no measure is readily available. Porter and Offenbacher devote considerable effort to getting around this unobservability problem. In fact, they take two different shots at avoiding this problem. I think they have failed on both counts.

Consider their first attempt, the direct procedure of estimating the brokerage fee. In this case, they use the two Miller-Orr equations: one for average money balances, the other for financial debits.

$$m = \alpha_{1h}\left(\frac{by^2}{r}\right)^{1/h} \tag{3.21}$$

$$d = \alpha_{2h}\left(\frac{\mathrm{ry}^4}{b}\right)^{1/h} \tag{3.22}$$

The two equations are written as *nonstochastic*, and both desired money balances (m) and financial debits (d) are stated as depending on interest rates (r), income (y), and the brokerage fee (b). All the variables in the two equations except the brokerage fee are known. Porter and Offenbacher solve these two equations for the brokerage fee in terms of the observable quantities: money balances, financial debits, income, and interest rates.

$$b = (r^2y^2/(d/m)^3)^{1/2} \tag{3.23}$$

This allows them to calculate a brokerage fee series that they, in turn, plug back into the original money demand equation 3.2. (Note that somehow this latter equation is now stochastic!) When Porter and Offenbacher estimate the money demand equation, they find that the coefficient on the brokerage fee variable is positive and significant, which in their eyes is highly encouraging.

Porter and Offenbacher, later on, do admit that there may be some suspicion of circularity in these results. This claim is quite generous. A more accurate description would be that the results are completely bankrupt with regard to determining the source of a shift in money demand. To see this, suppose there is an exogenous shift in money demand so that α_{1h} in equation 3.2 in the Porter-Offenbacher model is reduced. If we follow the Porter-Offenbacher procedure of estimating the brokerage fee, this derived brokerage fee series also will show a shift at that point. Thus, using their admittedly circular procedure, we would conclude incorrectly that the brokerage fee was responsible for the money demand shift, when in fact it was due to an exogenous shift. They have in essence forced the conclusion that brokerage fees explain the shift in money demand.

If we are more than suspicious of their findings at this point, what about their second attempt? The second attempt avoids this circularity problem. Instead of coming up with a direct estimate of the brokerage fee, Porter and Offenbacher proxy this variable with financial debits, which the Miller-Orr framework suggests is inversely related to the brokerage fee. Thus, they estimate a conventional money demand equation with financial debits as an additional explanatory variable. The coefficient on this variable turns out to be negative, as expected, and significant. Again, success is claimed.

In this second attempt, Porter and Offenbacher are guilty of ignoring their basic model. The Miller-Orr relationship between financial debits implies much more than the negative sign on that variable in the money demand equation on which Porter and Offenbacher focus. To understand this, rewrite equations 3.2 and 3.3 in log form

$$\ln M = \ln \alpha_{1h} + 1/h \ln b + 2/h \ln y - 1/h \ln r \qquad (3.24)$$

$$\ln d = \ln \alpha_{2h} + 1/h \ln r + 4/h \ln y - 1/h \ln b \qquad (3.25)$$

Solve equation 3.25 for ln b

$$\ln b = -h \ln d + h \ln \alpha_{2h} + \ln r + 4 \ln y$$

If this last expresion is substituted into equation 3.24 for b, we obtain

$$\ln M = (\ln \alpha_{1h} + \ln \alpha_{2h}) + 6/h \ln y - \ln d \qquad (3.26)$$

From this we see that if we include financial debits on the right-hand side of a money demand equation, their model says that interest rates should have no effect and the long-run elasticity with regard to financial debits should be unity. Their estimation results, however, reject both of the conclusions. Most disconcerting is the simultaneous significance of the coefficients on the financial debit and interest rate variables. Such a finding suggests they are capturing an effect for which they don't know the cause. Thus, rather than supporting the brokerage fee hypothesis, their findings necessitate rejection of their model. This is not to say we must reject the brokerage fee hypothesis itself. But it does suggest that Porter-Offenbacher have not provided any evidence in support of it.

Divisia Aggregation

This brings us to Porter and Offenbacher's second empirical sojourn—considering alternative means of aggregation. In the face of much empirical evidence, Porter and Offenbacher conclude that for aggregates broader than M1, the divisia method of aggregation is highly recommended. I would have to agree, based on evidence provided that for the broader aggregates, that weighted aggregation (or divisia aggregation) is preferable to simple sum aggregation, at least in terms of explaining the behavior of these variables from a demand equation framework. The only quibble I have with their evidence is that, in comparing the alternative aggregate demand relationships, they should have included all of the relevant opportunity cost variables as independent variables in the case of simple sum aggregation equations, when in fact they only include two interest rate variables. This would have avoided any degree of freedom bias in comparing simple sum aggregation with divisia aggregation, since the latter method requires knowledge of these many opportunity costs and the simple-sum money demand equations ignore such information.

My crude impression from the Porter-Offenbacher paper is that divisia aggregation represents nirvana. I would agree only to the extent that nirvana must be defined either in terms of a simple sum or divisia aggregation *for the broader aggregates*. I think the evidence provided by Porter and Offenbacher says that the broader monetary aggregates have encompassed financial assets that are not close substitutes for one another—indicating that when we aggregate across these assets, it is difficult to find a simple empirical demand relationship explaining that aggregate. I have always been suspect of the broader aggregates, and the Porter-Offenbacher paper confirms some of my suspicions.

To say that there are serious questions about the broader simple sum aggregates, however, does not imply that broader divisia aggregation represents a bliss point with regard to monetary policy. As an illustration of this point, I ask you to consider how the Federal Reserve would go about achieving a targeted growth rate for a divisia monetary aggregate. Recall that such an aggregate is a weighted average of many financial assets, with the weights changing each period with interest rates. In this regard, tomorrow's weights are unknown. Suffice it to say that if we have control problems today, they would greatly increase if we ever tried to control a divisia aggregate.

Conclusion

I think Porter and Offenbacher have failed in their effort to explain the breakdown in narrow money demand. They claim the breakdown is due to a specification error, but they provide only a vacuous test of this proposition or obtain results which necessitate rejection of their model. Most importantly from my perspective, however, they have not provided any evidence to suggest the breakdown is any more serious than the one-time shift Rik Hafer and I have found. In this regard, I remain a strong advocate of an M1 monetary target—not on theoretical, but empirical, grounds.

I don't take issue with their empirical support for the broader divisia aggregates as opposed to broader simple sum aggregates. They do provide evidence that raises serious questions about the broader simple-sum aggregates. Accepting this evidence though, I part company with them when it comes to the policy relevancy of their alternative—the divisia aggregate. Their analysis is limited to considering the relationship between an aggregate and economic activity. The issue of how well the Federal Reserve can achieve any desired level for such weighted aggregates is ignored.

References

Baumol, William J. "The Transactions Demand for Cash: An Inventory Theoretic Approach." *Quarterly Journal of Economics* (November 1952), 545–556.

Tobin, James. "The Interest Elasticity of the Transactions Demand for Cash." *Review of Economics and Statistics* (August 1956) 241–247.

4 FINANCIAL INNOVATION AND MONETARY TARGETING

Michael J. Hamburger

"If it ain't broke don't fix it."

Bert Lance
Spring 1977

The financial sector of the U.S. economy has been experiencing a wave of innovation which some observers have described as a veritable revolution. New financial instruments and services have been introduced and, in some instances, entirely new institutions (e.g., money market mutual funds) have been developed to provide these services. These changes have widespread implications for the competitive structure and market shares within the financial industry, the availability of financial services to the public, the distribution of financial risk, and the regulation of financial institutions. Most of the recent discussion, however, has focused on the implications of financial innovation for monetary policy, in particular the role of monetary targets in the implementation of policy.

In a speech to the American Economic and American Finance Associations, Anthony Solomon, President of the Federal Reserve Bank of New York, argued that financial innovation has important implications for the money measures that the Federal Reserve targets and for the levels at which the targets are set. Moreover, he suggested that in the long run, "the very viability of money stock targets is at stake" [Solomon, 1982].

More recently, Frank Morris, President of the Federal Reserve Bank of Boston, expressed similar reservations about the continued usefulness of monetary aggregate targets as guides for monetary policy. He stated that "the pace of innovation has led us to the point where any definition of the money supply must be arbitrary and unsatisfactory." And he concluded reluctantly that we can no longer measure the money supply with any kind of precision [Morris, 1982a, 1982b].

It should be noted that neither the innovations nor the concerns of policymakers are new. In January 1975, George Mitchell, Vice Chairman of the Federal Reserve Board, stated

> An end to the upward trend in the efficiency of money for transactions has been predicted for many years, but the evidence—statistical, institutional, and in money mores—has failed entirely thus far to support that expectation. To seek improved monetary control by reliance on a variable, M_1, whose characteristics are undergoing rapid change, involves unknown exposures. In my opinion, the concept of the narrowly defined money supply is becoming less and less appropriate even as a proxy for monetary action.

Despite these long-standing concerns, there has been relatively little research measuring the effects of financial innovation on the usefulness of monetary aggregate targets. One reason for this is the difficulty in quantifying financial innovations and their effects on financial markets. Most of the existing work focuses on the purported lack of stability of the demand function for money. While the stability of this function is obviously related to the usefulness of monetary targets, the two issues are not identical. It is conceivable that an empirically estimated demand function may cease to provide accurate forecasts of the amount of money the public wishes to hold, and yet changes in the stock of money could continue to be a good indicator of the future direction of the economy. One obvious example is where there is a change in the specification of some of the explanatory variables included in the demand function.

These issues are addressed in the second and third sections of this paper, which review existing research on the relationship between financial innovation and monetary targets. New evidence on this relationship is presented in the fourth section, while the fifth section provides a summary and a conclusion. Essentially, we wish to address two questions: (1) Has or will financial innovation impair the relationship between money and the real economy to reduce the usefulness of monetary aggregate targets? and (2) What are the best procedures to use in setting these targets? Before turning to this analysis, however, we will consider the effects of innovation on the composition of financial assets.

The Composition of Financial Assets

In the presence of high interest rates, financial innovation together with changes in banking legislation have led to dramatic changes in the way the public distributes its financial wealth. As illustrated in table 4–1, the last few years have witnessed almost explosive growth in money market mutual funds. In December 1978, the ratio of M1 to the balances in these funds was 51:1; it fell to 7:1 at the end of 1980; and, in August 1982, was 2.5:1.

The growth in other checkable deposits (primarily NOW accounts) is also impressive, although it has not been quite as fast as the growth of money market mutual funds. In December 1976, these deposits accounted for less than 1 percent of M1, rose to 4.3 percent in December 1979, 6.5 percent in December 1980, and in August were 19.8 percent. In the case of other checkable deposits, however, most of the growth has been at the expense of traditional demand deposits. In August, the sum of other checkables and demand deposits was 70.6 percent of M1, little changed from 70.9 percent in December 1980, and down only slightly from 73.2 percent in December 1976.[1] This would seem to affirm that the public treats other checkable

Table 4-1. M1 and Money Market Mutual Funds

	M1 ($ billions)	*Money Market Mutual Funds ($ billions)*	*Ratio of M1 to Money Market Funds*	*Percent of M1 held as:* Demand Deposits	Other Checkables
Dec. 1976	310.4	2.8	111:1	72.3	0.9
Dec. 1977	335.5	2.9	115:1	71.4	1.2
Dec. 1978	363.2	7.1	51:1	69.9	2.3
Dec. 1979	389.0	34.4	11:1	67.4	4.3
Dec. 1980	414.5	61.9	6.7:1	64.5	6.5
Dec. 1981	440.9	151.2	2.9:1	53.6	17.5
Aug. 1982	455.2	180.0	2.5:1	50.8	19.8

Table 4-2. Composition of M2

		Percent held as		
	M2 ($ billions)	*M1*	*Saving and Small-time Deposits*	*Money Market Funds, Overnight RPs, and Eurodollars*
Jan. 1977	1,184	26.5	72.6	1.3
Dec. 1977	1,298	25.8	72.8	1.7
Dec. 1978	1,404	25.9	72.2	2.2
Dec. 1979	1,519	25.6	70.7	4.0
Dec. 1980	1,656	25.0	69.5	5.8
Dec. 1981	1,823	24.2	65.7	10.4
Aug. 1982	1,946	23.4	65.4	11.6

deposits as transaction balances and argues for aggregating these deposits together with traditional demand deposits. The rapid growth in the share of other checkables in 1981 which apparently has not continued in 1982 suggests that these deposits are preferable for some people, but not for everyone.

The composition of M2 has also been affected by financial innovation, but here the changes have been more modest (table 4–2). In January 1977, practically all of M2 was held either in M1 (26.5%) or savings and small time deposits (72.6%). By August 1982, the growth in money market mutual funds plus overnight Eurodollars and overnight Repurchase Agreements (RPs) had caused each of these shares to fall by about 10 percent.[2]

While these trends in the distribution of assets provide the necessary perspective for analyzing financial innovation, most monetary policy studies focus on the behavior of alternative measures of the velocity of money. Of particular interest is the velocity of the narrow definition of money, M1, which is generally viewed as being the most susceptible to variabilities arising because of financial innovation.

Velocity and the Demand for Money

The ultimate objectives of monetary policy are to reduce inflation, promote economic growth, and contribute to a sustainable pattern of international transactions. In framing short-run decisions, the Federal Reserve tends to rely on its ability to influence the growth of nominal income to achieve the ultimate policy objectives. Monetary growth targets may be used to achieve the desired growth in income, *if* the velocity of money is predictable. For example:

$$\dot{Y} = \dot{M} + \dot{V} \qquad (4.1)$$

where $\dot{Y}$ is the growth of nominal income
$\dot{M}$ is the growth of money
$\dot{V}$ is the growth of velocity.

Hence, it is generally agreed that the usefulness of monetary aggregate targets depends on the accuracy of velocity growth predictions.

In the present policy environment, the Federal Reserve sets monetary growth targets over four-quarter periods. If the standard error of velocity growth predictions over these periods is 1 percentage point (and is independent of monetary growth), the Federal Reserve would be able to do reasonably well in achieving desired income growth. In that case, the four-quarter growth rate of nominal GNP would fall between $\pm$ 1 percent of its desired rate two-thirds of the time.

A number of studies of the demand for money have concluded that financial innovation is undermining the accuracy of velocity predictions. A recent example is the work of Higgins and Faust (1981), in which a velocity equation is derived from a money-demand function estimated from 1959:2 to 1974:2.[3] The effect of financial innovation on velocity predictions is then determined by the equation's inability to explain movements in velocity beyond the sample period of 1974:3 to 1981:2.

The demand function for M1 money balances used in this study is of the form

$$\log(M1_t/P_t) = A_0 + A_1 \log y_t + A_2 \log r_t + A_3 \log(M1_{t-1}/P_t) \qquad (4.2)$$

where y is GNP in constant (1972) dollars
P is the GNP deflator
r is the opportunity cost of holding money, measured by one or more interest rates.

To convert this function to a velocity relationship, both sides of equation 4.2 are subtracted from the logarithm of nominal GNP (Y) to yield

$$\log V_t = \log Y_t - \log M1_t = -A_0 + (1-A_1) \log y_t - A_2 \log r_t - A_3 \log(M1_{t-1}/P_t) \qquad (4.3)$$

Table 4-3. Actual and Predicted Levels of M1 and M1 Velocity from Dynamic Simulations of M1 Demand Functions

	M1[a] ($ billions or percent)			*M1 Velocity[b]*		
	Actual	*Predicted*	*Percentage Error*	*Actual*	*Predicted*	*Percentage Error*
1974:4	282.1	290.1	−2.8	5.33	5.28	0.9
1975:4	295.1	317.0	−6.9	5.59	5.33	4.9
1976:4	312.1	344.8	−9.5	5.75	5.31	8.3
1977:4	336.9	374.3	−10.0	5.97	5.43	9.9
1978:4	361.4	406.5	−11.1	6.32	5.73	10.3
1979:4	N/A	N/A	N/A	6.46	5.82	11.0
1980:4	N/A	N/A	N/A	6.59	5.93	11.1

[a]Reproduced from Porter, Simpson, and Mauskopf (1979, p. 214). Percentage errors are the actual values minus the predictions as a percent of the predictions.

[b]Derived from Higgins and Faust (1981, table 1, p. 9). The values shown here were supplied by the authors and are based on revised data as of August 1982. Percentage errors calculated as above.

Since equations 4.2 and 4.3 are linear transformations of one another, their estimating and predictive properties are the same. Hence, the results obtained by Higgins and Faust for M1 velocity should correspond to those in studies of the demand for M1, which employ the same demand function and a similar estimation period.

The left side of table 4–3 provides the typical pattern of out-of-sample residuals for conventional M1-demand functions fit through mid-1974.[4] As is well known, such results suggest a significant downward shift in the demand for money beginning in 1974. By 1976:4, actual holdings of M1 were 9.5 percent below the level derived from the demand function fitted to pre-1974 data. Over the next two years, the gap between predicted and actual money holdings widened further, although the rate of deterioration in the predictive ability of the equation did moderate somewhat. By 1978:4, the actual level of M1 was 11.1 percent below that expected on the basis of the estimated demand function.

The Higgins-Faust velocity analysis is also based on a conventional money-demand function. As the authors indicate, its only unconventional aspect is that, instead of measuring the opportunity cost of holding money by one or more short-term interest rates, it uses a weighted average of several rates: the federal funds rate, the passbook savings rate, the 3-month Treasury bill rate, the commercial paper rate, the 5-year government bond rate, the 20-year government bond rate, and the dividend-price ratio on common stocks. Given the number of short-term interest rates included, it seems likely that their movements will dominate those of the Higgins-Faust weighted average. Consequently, it is not surprising that the behavior of the Higgins-Faust velocity equation beyond its 1959:2–1974:2 sample period corresponds closely to the money-demand results discussed above. As shown on the right side of table 4–3, actual M1 velocity in 1976:4 exceeds its predicted value by 8.3 percent, implying a sustantial decline in the amount of money held by the public for given levels of income and interest rates. Extending the postsample period beyond 1976:4 has the same effect as it does in the money-demand studies; the gap between the predicted and actual level of velocity widens to 10.3 percent in 1978:4 and to 11.1 percent in 1980:4.

The conclusion generally drawn from these results is that financial innovation creates major problems for the continued use of monetary aggregate targets. For example, Higgins and Faust argue

> The new monetary aggregates have exhibited . . . erratic velocity behavior recently, thereby posing serious problems for monetary policy implementation. Continuing rapid financial innovation may . . . continue to impair the reliability of traditional money-demand relationships used to predict velocity. . . . If this is correct, it may be necessary to reevaluate the desirability of using monetary aggregate targets to achieve ultimate policy objectives [Higgins and Faust, 1981].

Porter, Simpson, and Mauskopf (1979) claim

> Financial innovations . . . present a number of difficulties for the interpretation of the monetary aggregates and for the conduct of monetary policy. Some of these difficulties can be reduced by changing the definitions of the monetary aggregates. . . . However, given the unpredictable timing and size of the shifts in M1 demand, it is likely that even the best adjustments will be off the mark. In such an environment, it is more important than ever that policymakers supplement information on monetary aggregates with data on near-money and other financial assets, interest rates, and direct indicators of current and future developments in the economy.

Despite its popularity, this conclusion is seriously flawed; it ignores a variety of evidence which suggests that the recent behavior of M1 velocity is not significantly different from that prior to 1974. The next section presents evidence derived from an alternative formulation of the demand for money. The fourth section examines the behavior of velocity independent of a particular specification of the demand function. This permits an investigation of the appropriateness of M1 as a policy target, even in the absence of agreement on the proper specification of its demand function.

An Alternative Money-Demand Function

Previously I estimated an alternative demand function for M1 which differs from the conventional formulation in one crucial respect; it does not include any interest rates on short-term marketable financial instruments as components of the opportunity cost of holding money. Instead, the opportunity cost of holding money is measured by the interest rate on savings deposits, the yield on long-term government bonds, and the dividend-price ratio on common stocks, each taken as a separate variable. The rationale for this specification was that

> the long-term bond rate is included on the assumption that: (a) most financial assets are substitutes for money and (b) during the period under consideration it may be more representative of all the relevant yields than [a short-term] rate. (Multicolinearity problems make it difficult to include interest rates on both short-term and long-term financial assets in the same equation.) The dividend-price ratio is taken as the yield on equities (claims on the earnings and real assets of firms), but may be viewed as an indicator of the yield on all physical capital [Hamburger, 1977].[5]

Over the period for which the function was originally estimated 1955:2–1972:4, use of a long-term interest rate as opposed to a short-term rate (e.g., the Treasury bill rate) yields a slightly poorer statistical fit; the standard errors of estimate for the level of M1 are 0.47 percent and 0.41 percent, respectively. (See Hamburger, 1977, p. 276, footnote 16.) However, for the postsample period beginning in mid-1974, the function which incorporates both the long-term bond rate and the yield on equities suffers from none of the problems that beset the conventional demand function. Indeed, the dynamic simulation results shown in table 4–4 suggest that this function fits the post-1974:2 period about as well as it does the sample period. The errors alternate in sign and the largest single error is only 1.9 percent. In short, there is no indication of a shift in the function or any deterioration in the accuracy of velocity predictions.[6]

The question that naturally arises is why should two formulations of the demand for money that perform about equally well from the mid-1950s to the early 1970s suddenly behave so differently? Why should a specification using long-term interest rates continue to fit as well as it did before, while

Table 4-4. Actual and Predicted Levels of M1 from Dynamic Simulations of an Alternative M1 Demand Function*

	Actual M1	*Predicted M1*	*Percentage Error*
1974:4	$274.7	$273.6	0.4
1975:4	288.2	288.7	−0.2
1976:4	305.1	312.1	−1.9
1977:4	330.3	335.3	−1.5
1978:4	357.4	358.7	−0.4
1979:4	384.8	384.0	0.2
1980:4	413.0	406.3	1.6

*Based on actual M1 data as of February 1981.

Estimated Demand Function:
1955:2 to 1974:2
(t-statistics in parentheses)

$$\begin{aligned}\text{Log}\,(\text{M1/Y}) = \underset{(1.73)}{.032} - \underset{(2.41)}{.018}\,\text{Log DP} - \underset{(2.01)}{.016}\,\text{Log RTD} - \underset{(2.23)}{.023}\,\text{Log RGB} \\ + \underset{(41.42)}{0.918}\,\text{Log}\,(\text{M1/Y})\end{aligned}$$

$R^2 = 0.9980$ SE = .0047 DW = 1.85 RHO = 0.36

where

DP is the dividend price rate
RTD is the rate on time deposits
RGB is the yield on long-term government bonds

specifications employing short-term rates go significantly off-track? One possible explanation is financial innovation. The effects of some of the most significant innovations have been to reduce the transaction costs associated with short-term credit market instruments. Thus, shares in money market mutual funds (and to some extent overnight RPs) may be viewed as Treasury bills or negotiable CDs with substantially lower transaction costs. One result is that small investors have been able to enter the negotiable CD market and to once again hold Treasury bills.

This means that for any observed level of market interest rates the net return on short-term credit instruments (i.e., the gross yield less transaction costs) will be higher than it was prior to the innovations. Consequently, if transaction costs are not taken into account, one would find that for given levels of short-term interest rates investors would hold more securities and less money than they did before. While this explanation is obviously speculative, it reflects the results obtained with so-called conventional money-demand functions. These functions use short-term interest rates to measure the opportunity cost of holding money, make no allowance for changing transaction costs, and since 1974 have substantially overpredicted desired money holdings. The implication is that these overpredictions are not due to instabilities in the underlying behavior of velocity, but rather to the misspecification of the opportunity cost of holding money.

Ordinarily, the use of short-term interest rates to measure the opportunity cost of holding money might not be a problem. However, as a result of financial innovation there is reason to question whether observed short-term rates provide a continuous and unbiased time series of these costs. No similar problem occurs for long-term rates; money-demand functions using these rates fit the recent data about as well as the past.[7]

The Behavior of Velocity

In view of the potential problems of choosing among alternative money-demand functions, it is useful to examine the behavior of M1 velocity independent of the constraints imposed by specific formulations of these functions. If velocity is becoming more erratic, either because of financial innovation or any other reason, one might expect a change in its trend rate of growth, an increase in the deviations around trend, or both.

The proliferation of money substitutes (money market mutual funds, overnight RPs, etc.) and new banking services (deposit sweeping) has led some to expect an acceleration in the trend growth of velocity; for example, see Porter, Simpson, and Mauskopf (1979) and Cagan (1982). On the other hand, there was some expectation that the nationwide legalization of NOW accounts in January 1981 might increase the demand for M1 and reduce velocity growth. The FOMC apparently accepted this line of reasoning and specified monetary growth targets for 1981 on the assumption that the introduction of NOW accounts would lower the growth of M1 velocity by 2½ percentage points [Board of Governors, Federal Reserve System, 1981].

Table 4–5 records the annual growth rates of nominal GNP, M1, and the velocity of M1, calculated on a fourth-quarter to fourth-quarter basis, as is appropriate given the Federal Reserve's present targeting procedures. As

Table 4-5. Growth Rate of Nominal GNP and M1*

	Growth Rate of Nominal GNP	*Growth Rate of M1*	*Growth Rate of Velocity of M1*	*Standard Deviation of Annual M1 Velocity Growth*
1954–80	7.8	4.5	3.1	1.8
1961–80	8.8	5.5	3.1	1.7
1954–60	4.8	1.7	3.1	1.9
1961–70	7.2	4.3	2.8	2.0
1971–80	10.5	6.8	3.5	1.4
1971–75	10.0	6.1	3.6	1.3
1976–80	11.1	7.5	3.4	1.4
1954	3.4	2.6	0.9	
1955	9.4	2.4	6.8	
1956	5.1	1.1	4.0	
1957	2.8	−0.3	3.0	
1958	5.2	3.3	1.8	
1959	6.0	2.1	3.8	
1960	2.0	0.5	1.5	
1961	7.5	2.7	4.5	
1962	5.8	1.8	4.0	
1963	6.6	4.0	2.5	
1964	5.9	4.4	1.5	
1965	10.5	4.4	5.9	
1966	8.0	2.8	5.1	
1967	6.2	6.4	−0.1	
1968	9.4	7.4	1.9	
1969	6.8	3.9	2.9	
1970	4.9	4.9	0.0	
1971	9.6	6.7	2.7	
1972	11.6	8.5	2.8	
1973	11.6	5.8	5.5	
1974	7.0	4.8	2.2	
1975	10.0	5.0	4.8	
1976	9.3	6.2	2.9	
1977	12.2	8.2	3.7	
1978	14.7	8.2	6.0	
1979	9.7	7.4	2.1	
1980	9.4	7.3	2.0	
1981	9.6	5.0	4.4	

*Old M1 growth from 1954–59; new M1 growth from 1960–81.

was the case in the previous section, these data do not support the view that the behavior of velocity has become more erratic.

First, there is no indication of any significant change in the trend growth of velocity. It is true that from 1975 to 1980 the growth in M1 velocity was higher than in the 1960s. But this represented a deceleration from slightly faster growth in the 1971–75 period and was only marginally above the growth in the late 1950s. Essentially, the data indicate that the 5- and 10-year growth rates of M1 velocity vary narrowly around the 1954–80 trend of 3.1 percent. Second, the year-to-year fluctuations in the growth of M1 velocity are also small; and, as the standard deviations (in the right-hand column) reveal, the growth in M1 velocity was more stable in the 1970s than it was before.[8]

Finally, a look at the most recent data should also help to dispel some of the concern about the impact of new financial instruments on the demand for money and the behavior of velocity. In 1979 and 1980, when money market mutual funds really began to gain popularity, the growth of M1 velocity (2.1%) was somewhat below its long-run average of 3.1 percent. This is clearly not what would have happened if the new instruments were being used as alternatives to conventional money. In that case, M1 velocity would have grown very rapidly. Some of this shortfall was made up in 1981 as the growth in velocity spurted to 4.4 percent. But once again a number of analysts were caught by surprise, as they expected the introduction of NOW accounts to spur the growth in M1 and depress velocity.

The implication is that the year-to-year growth in M1 velocity is a well-behaved random variable which can be predicted with relatively little error, even in the absence of an econometrically estimated money-demand function. Since 1970 its value has fallen between ±1.4 percent of the average growth over this period (3.4%).

Conclusion

Two questions were raised at the outset: (1) Has or will financial innovation impair the relationship between money and the real economy so as to reduce the usefulness of monetary aggregate targets? and (2) What are the best procedures to use in setting aggregate targets? Contrary to the results of some conventional money-demand studies, the preponderance of evidence for the last quarter-century suggests that the answer to the first question is no. There is no indication of any recent deterioration in the relationship between the growth in M1 and GNP. If anything, the year-to-year growth in M1 velocity was more stable in the 1970s than from 1954 through 1970.

The evidence bearing on alternative target-setting procedures is less definitive. Nevertheless, one point is clear: the only studies that encounter any problem in explaining recent velocity movements are those based on so-called conventional money-demand function, i.e., those which use short-term interest rates to measure the opportunity cost of holding money. As argued above, the problem could be that financial innovation has distorted the meaning of these rates. Regardless of the explanation, though, the evidence strongly suggests that one should be leery about using short-term interest rates as guides for monetary policy. The yield velocity growth projections that are less accurate than those obtained by extrapolating past trends. In this context, it is disconcerting to note that legislation is currently pending in Congress (S. 2807, the Balanced Monetary Policy Act of 1982) which would require the Federal Reserve to set targets for short-term real interest rates as well as the monetary and credit aggregates. It would seem incumbent on those who propose such legislation to demonstrate empirically that this would improve the conduct of policy and contribute to the stability of the economy. All existing evidence suggest that it would not.

Long-term interest rates and common stock yields appear to have been less affected by financial innovation than short-term rates. As a result, functions that use these rates to measure the opportunity cost of holding money continue to provide accurate explanations of velocity movements. However, use of these relationships for target-setting purposes requires forecasts of asset yields one year ahead. In view of the obvious difficulties in forecasting interest rates, it would seem more prudent to rely on the extrapolation of past trends in velocity growth, certainly until there is convincing evidence that the trend growth rate has changed or that fluctuations around trend have increased substantially. At present, such evidence does not exist.

Notes

1. Moreover, the decline from 1976 to 1980 was smaller than that from 1972 to 1976 (76.9% vs. 73.2%). The major cause of both changes is the currency drain, which is ongoing.

2. Within the savings and small time deposit category there has also been a significant shift away from savings deposits. Partially as a result of this, M2 now responds very differently to the business cycle.

3. Another study using the same methodology and obtaining similar results is that of Kopcke and Dockser (1982), which provided the empirical basis for Morris' (1982) views.

4. The form of these functions is similar to equation 4.2. They have come to be viewed as conventional because: (1) the quantity of money explained is the real money stock—money balances relative to the average price of goods and services—rather than nominal (current dollar) money balances; (2) lagged real money balances are included as an explanatory variable

to allow for a distributed lag adjustment of actual money balances to their determinants, real income, and interest rates; and (3) the principal interest rates used to measure the opportunity cost of holding money are those on short-term credit instruments, because these assets are assumed to be the closest substitutes for money. The results shown in table 4–3 are taken from Porter, Simpson, and Mauskopf (1979); essentially identical results are reported by Goldfeld (1976) and Enzler, Johnson, and Paulus (1976).

5. At the time, the possibility of using a weighted average of a number of interest rates, as is done by Higgins and Faust, was not considered.

6. Despite the close statistical fit of this alternative M1-demand function during the periods both before and after 1974, some of its properties remain the subject of controversy. One question concerns the appropriateness of using the dividend-price ratio to measure the return on equities. Judd and Scadding (1982) argue that the measure fails to include expected capital gains in the numerator. Moreover, Benjamin M. Friedman (1978) claims that the dividend-price ratio serves as a proxy for wealth, since most of its movements come from the price term, which is correlated with wealth. However, both of these questions were addressed in Hamburger (1966, p. 606, footnote 9), where it was shown that they had no bearing on the performance of the function. Others, such as Hafer and Hein (1979), argue that the function's superiority in forecasting post-1974 data is heavily dependent on a restriction on the long-run real income elasticity that is not supported by the sample period data. As implied in the lower half of table 3–4, the equation constrains both the long-run price and real income elasticities to equal one. However, Hafer and Hein (1979, p. 7) show that if the long-run real income elasticity is estimated freely, its value is significantly less than 1.0. The problem with this demonstration is that Hafer and Hein elsewhere show (1979, p. 10) that the equation with the unconstrained real income elasticity is unstable during the sample period, while the constrained equation is stable in both the sample and postsample periods. Moreover, the difference in the postsample predictive power of the two equations is relatively small.

7. Hafer and Hein (1982) argue that the principal problem with the conventional money-demand function is that it fails to allow for a once-and-for-all downward level shift in 1974:2. But their own results do not fully support this view. Equation 4.2 shows that if the conventional function is altered to allow for only an intercept shift, it is statistically significant. On the other hand, when all of the parameters are permitted to change in 1974:2 (which would seem to be the relevant test), the intercept shift is no longer significant.

8. In the present policy environment, it is appropriate to calculate velocity growth on a fourth-quarter to fourth-quarter basis. However, as shown in Weintraub (1981) and in Republican Members Joint Economic Committee (1982) almost identical results are obtained when the calculations are based on calendar-year averages.

References

Board of Governors of the Federal Reserve System. *Monetary Policy Report to Congress Pursuant to the Full Employment and Balanced Growth Act of 1978*, February 25, 1981.

Cagan, Phillip. "The Choice Among Monetary Aggregates as Targets and Guides for Monetary Policy." *Journal of Money, Credit and Banking* (November, 1982).

Enzler, Jared, Lewis Johnson, and John Paulus. "Some Problems of Money Demand." *Brookings Papers on Economic Activity* (1976:1), 261–280.

Friedman, Benjamin M. "The Case of the Missing Money." *Brookings Papers on Economic Activity* (1978:3), 593–641.

Goldfeld, Stephen M. "The Case of the Missing Money." *Brookings Papers on Economic Activity* (1976:3), 683–730.

Hafer, R. W. and Scott E. Hein. "Evidence on the Temporal Stability of the Demand for Money Relationship in the United States." *Review* Federal Reserve Bank of St. Louis (December 1979), 3–14.

Hafer, R. W. and Scott E. Hein. "The Shift in Money Demand: What Really Happened?" *Review* Federal Reserve Bank of St. Louis (February 1982), 11–16.

Hamburger, Michael J. "The Demand for Money by Households, Money Substitutes, and Monetary Policy." *Journal of Political Economy* (December 1966), 600–623.

Hamburger, Michael J. "Behavior of the Money Stock: Is There a Puzzle?" *Journal of Monetary Economics* (July 1977), 265–288.

Higgins, Bryon and Jon Faust. "Velocity Behavior of the New Monetary Aggregates." *Economic Review* Federal Reserve Bank of Kansas City (September-October 1981), 3–17.

The Joint Economic Committee. "Republican Views," Chapter 4. *The 1982 Joint Economic Report* (March 1, 1982).

Judd, John P. and John L. Scadding. "The Search for a Stable Money Demand Function: A Survey of the Post-1973 Literature." *Journal of Economic Literature* (September 1982).

Kopcke, Richard W. and Mark Dockser. "Appendix" to "Do the Monetary Aggregates Have a Future as Targets of Federal Reserve Policy?" *New England Economic Review*, Federal Reserve Bank of Boston (March/April 1982), 12–14.

Mitchell, G. W. "Inflation and the Federal Reserve." Remarks at the Conference on the State of the Economy, College of Business Administration, the University of Iowa, January 15, 1975.

Morris, Frank. "Do the Monetary Aggregates Have a Future as Targets of Federal Reserve Policy?" *New England Economic Review*, Federal Reserve Bank of Boston (March/April 1982), 5–11.

Morris, Frank. "A Fed President Views the Money Supply." *Wall Street Journal*, June 22, 1982.

Porter, Richard D., Thomas Simpson, and Eileen Mauskopf. "Financial Innovation and the Monetary Aggregates." *Brookings Papers on Economic Activity* (1979:1), 213–229.

Solomon, Anthony M. "New Strategies for the Federal Reserve?" *Challenge* (March-April, 1982), 18–24. The article was a speech delivered to a joint luncheon of the American Economic and Finance Associations, December 28, 1981, Washington, D.C.

Weintraub, Robert E. *Deficits: Their Impact on Inflation and Growth*. The Joint Economic Committee, July 30, 1981.

DISCUSSION

Laurence H. Meyer

Michael Hamburger's paper reminds us that there are two puzzles associated with empirical money demand equations in the post-1973 period. The first puzzle is why the conventional (Goldfeld) specification breaks down. The second puzzle is why Mike Hamburger's specification does not.

But the first puzzle—the breakdown of the conventional equation—seems less of a mystery when we recognize the perhaps unprecedented pace of financial innovation and institutional change over the last 10 to 15 years, affecting both the availability money substitutes and the transactions costs associated with moving into and out of money substitutes, and hence the net returns available on liquid alternatives to money. Particularly in light of the failure of empirical money demand equations to explicitly account for changes in the transactions costs associated with moving between money and nonmoney liquid financial assets, it is not surprising that the conventional equation overpredicts money demand after 1973. That leaves us with one puzzle: the immunity displayed by Hamburger's specification.

The out-of-sample performance of Hamburger's equation is unquestionably impressive. Perhaps the most impressive feature of Hamburger's econometrics is that he didn't allow his equation to get confused by the data over the sample period. The data, for example, argued forcefully that the income elasticity of money demand was significantly less than unity; but Hamburger opted, fortuitously it turned out, for a unitary income elasticity. The data also suggested the inclusion of an open market short-term interest rate and questioned the relevance of the long-term interest rate. But, again fortuitously, he ignored the data, excluded the short rate, and included the long rate. As Rik Hafer and Scott Hein have documented (1979), each of these decisions to impose restrictions not justified by the sample data improved the equation's out-of-sample performance. Any mortal econometrician can listen to the data. It takes something more (or, some might say, less) to ignore the data.

Given the imposition of restrictions inconsistent with the sample data, it was easy initially to push Hamburger's equation aside and to suppose that its remarkable performance was an aberration that would not persist. But it did, and for the better part of a decade since 1973. So we can no longer ignore it.

Hamburger's paper develops two themes. First, he attempts to explain why the conventional empirical money demand equation has broken down while his specification continues to perform well. Second, Hamburger presents evidence that the breakdown in the conventional equation has not been associated with either faster or more variable velocity growth nor with other evidence of a weakening or change in the relation between the money supply and economic activity. His conclusion is that nothing has occurred in the post-1973 period to weaken the case for monetary aggregate targeting.

I will consider each of these themes and his conclusion in turn. But I should note at the outset that I find the two themes incompatible. Hamburger's explanation of the money demand puzzle is that there was a significant decline in the transactions costs associated with moving into and out of short-term nonmoney financial assets. There will, I expect, be widespread agreement that such a change in transactions costs is an important factor in the explanation of the breakdown of the conventional equation. But such a development should have induced an attempt to economize on money and, therefore, should have generated an increase in velocity. If the pattern of velocity since 1973 does not indicate such a change, there is reason to question Hamburger's explanation of the breakdown in the conventional equation. As it turns out, his explanation makes good sense; it is his interpretation of velocity behavior after 1973 that is questionable. I conclude with some comments on the implications of the behavior of money demand and velocity for the wisdom of monetary aggregate targeting.

Explaining the Breakdown in the Conventional Equation

In his *Journal of Monetary Economics* paper (1977), Hamburger views the superior performance of his specification as evidence supporting the monetarist asset model and rejecting the Keynesian transaction model of money demand.

> The issue here is not a technical econometric one involving the appropriate measure of certain independent variables. . . . Monetarists have consistently objected to the transactions approach to money demand which limits the class of assets viewed as money substitutes to very short-term financial assets. For them, money is an effective substitute for many assets, both real and financial (p. 272).

He goes on to argue that the post-1973 instability in conventional (transactions-based) money-demand equations reflects the restriction imposed by the transactions models on the relevant set of interest rates in the money-demand function. He concludes that the stability of his specification is "consistent with our more general wealth adjustment or portfolio balance approach to the demand for money, but stands in strong opposition to the Keynesian or transactions approach" (p. 274).

I expect few were persuaded that the problem with the conventional equation was its failure to allow for substitutions between money and long-term bonds and equities. Indeed, there emerged widespread agreement that the instability in the conventional money-demand equation was linked to the increased availability and attractiveness of short-term financial assets and to improved cash management techniques—events well within the scope of the transactions model. In the current paper, Hamburger seems to have reversed his position; he now suggests that the divergent performance of the conventional equation and his specification *is* due to a technical econometric [problem] involving the appropriate measure of certain econometric variables, specifically to the failure of empirical transactions equations to include a measure of transactions costs associated with moving into and out of short-term nonmoney financial assets.

To develop the implications of a change in transactions costs, we begin by writing the conventional theoretical specification of the transactions model as

$$\ln m = a_0 + a_1 \ln \text{TCS} + a_2 \ln \text{RST} + a_3 \ln y \qquad (4.5)$$

where m is real money demand, TCS is transactions costs associated with short-term financial assets (as a percent of funds invested); RST is the (gross) rate on a representative short-term open market asset; y is real income; and $a_1 > 0$, $a_2 < 0$, and $a_3 > 0$ according to the transactions model. Traditionally, we subsume the transactions cost term in the constant; e.g., $a_0' = a_0 + a_1 \text{TCS}$. This is, of course, appropriate if real transactions costs are constant (and we could easily accommodate a steady decline in real transactions costs with a time trend in the equation). Hamburger interprets the events of the post-1973 period as yielding a dramatic decline in real transactions costs. This decline should decrease the demand for money, given that $a_1 > 0$ according to the transactions model. Failure to account for this decline in transactions costs resulted in the systematic overprediction of money demand after 1973.

Alternatively we could combine the TCS and RST terms into a net return variable (RST^{N})

$$\text{RST}^{\text{N}} = \text{RST} - \text{TCS}. \tag{4.6}$$

In terms of this variable, the interpretation of recent financial innovations is that the net return available to wealth owners on short-term assets has increased and this has resulted in a decline in desired money holdings. Money market mutual funds and overnight Repurchase Agreements, in particular, are highly liquid, pay interest rates close to rates on commercial paper and CDs, but have lower transactions costs associated with entry and exit and, therefore, offer higher net yields as part of a transactions portfolio.

This seems a reasonable explanation of the breakdown in the conventional equation. Judd and Scadding (1982) reach a similar conclusion in their recent survey of post-1973 empirical work on money demand. But why does Hamburger's specification remain well-behaved? To develop his explanation, let me introduce a simple term structure equation, relating net long-term rate to net short-term rates

$$\text{RLT} - \text{TCL} = g\ (\text{RST} - \text{TCS}) \tag{4.7}$$

The term structure equation is the link between the conventional equation, employing a short rate, and Hamburger's equation, using long-term rates. Over periods where real transactions costs are stable, a similar relation to equation 4.7 will hold between gross long and short rates. This explains the finding that gross short and long rates, if not interchangeable, both perform adequately in money demand equations in the pre-1973 period.

Hamburger notes, however, that the financial innovations which have lowered transactions costs associated with nonmoney short-term financial assets have not altered the transactions costs associated with long-term financial assets. With TCL fixed, RLT and RLT^N (RLT − TCL) are interchangeable in the term structure equation; but with TCS declining, gross and net long rates should rise relative to gross short-term rates. The gross long-term rate will continue to proxy the net short-term rate. The decline in TCS, which is not accounted for in the conventional equation, is captured by the upward movement in the gross long-term rate (relative to the gross short-term rate) in the Hamburger specification; this results in a decline in money demand in Hamburger's specification, preventing it from systematically overpredicting money demand.

If this explanation is correct, we should be able to identify a shift in the empirical term structure relation in the post-1973 period. To determine if this occurred, we estimate a simple term structure equation

$$\text{RLT} = b_0 + b_1\,\text{RST} + b_2\,\text{DUMMY} + b_3\,\text{RLT}_{-1} \qquad (4.8)$$

over the 1960I–1980IV period, where RLT is measured by the AAA corporate bond rate and RST by the commercial paper rate, and where DUMMY is 0 prior to 1974I and 1 in 1974I and thereafter. We run a similar equation for the relation between RDP, the dividend price ratio, and the short-term rate.

The estimated equations are

$$\underset{}{\text{RLT}_t} = \underset{(0.79)}{0.095} + \underset{(9.00)}{0.14}\,\text{RST}_t + \underset{(32.31)}{0.86}\,\text{RLT}_{t-1} + \underset{(1.46)}{0.13}\,\text{DUMMY} \qquad (4.9)$$

$R^2 = .99$

$dw = 1.96$

$$\text{RDP}_t = \underset{(3.84)}{0.83} + \underset{(3.44)}{0.052}\,\text{RST}_t + \underset{(9.60)}{0.66}\,\text{RDP}_{t-1} + \underset{(3.07)}{0.37}\,\text{DUMMY} \qquad (4.10)$$

$R^2 = .88$

$rho = 0.34$

These results give some support to the hypothesis that there was a shift in the relation between gross short and long rates in a direction consistent with the Hamburger explanation. The increase in the intercept of the long-term interest rate equation is only significant at the 15 percent level. The increase in the intercept of the RDP equation, however, is larger and significant at the 1 percent level. I conclude that Hamburger's current explanation for the divergent behavior of the conventional equation is plausible, receives some modest support from evidence on the term structure, and, in particular, is much more plausible than the explanation in his earlier paper.

Financial Innovations, Money Demand, and Velocity

The second theme in Hamburger's paper is that there has been no change in the behavior of velocity in the post-1973 period. But the financial innovations that resulted in the breakdown of the conventional equation should have affected velocity behavior. The decline in money demand they induced should have been translated to an increase in velocity. But Hamburger concludes that "there is no indication of any significant change in the trend growth of velocity" and that velocity "was more stable in the 1970s than it was before."

It is particularly discouraging if we cannot agree on something as simple as whether or not velocity grew more rapidly after 1973. But, alas, apparently we cannot. Hamburger computes annual velocity growth rates based on changes from fourth quarter to fourth quarter. His conclusions are based on growth rates and standard deviations over the periods in 1971–1975 and 1976–1980; these are reproduced in table 4–6 from Hamburger's paper. Based on these figures, Hamburger concludes that velocity growth has not accelerated in the period of rapid financial innovations.

I chose to break the period on the basis of evidence on the timing of the onset of money demand instability: the first period is from 1960I–1973IV, a period over which the conventional money demand specification is stable; the second period is from 1974I–1980IV, the period over which the conventional equation systematically overpredicts money demand. The mean growth rates and standard deviations for the two periods are given in table 4–7. The growth rate in velocity is about 15 percent higher in the second period. The standard deviation is also larger in the second period, again by about 15 percent.

Table 4-6. Growth Rate in Velocity Over Selected Periods

	Growth Rate	*Standard Deviation*
1954–60	3.1	1.9
1961–70	2.8	2.0
1971–75	3.6	1.3
1976–80	3.3	1.4

Table 4-7. Growth Rate in Velocity

	Mean	*Standard Deviation*
60I–73IV	2.87	3.19
74I–80IV	3.32	3.69
60I–80IV	3.02	3.34

Hamburger computes velocity growth rates over four- to five-year periods. I plot the 20 quarter growth rates for velocity over the 1970I–1981IV period in figure 4–1 (see also table 4–8); a vertical line is drawn at 1973IV, marking the approximate point of the shift based on evidence from conventional money demand functions. The picture shows clearly the move to a higher trend rate of growth in velocity after 1973.

We can follow this up by looking at simple velocity regressions against a time trend, including a one-time level shift dummy and/or a dummy for a change in the growth rate. It is important to determine whether the change in velocity behavior is a one-time level shift or a change in the growth rate. This

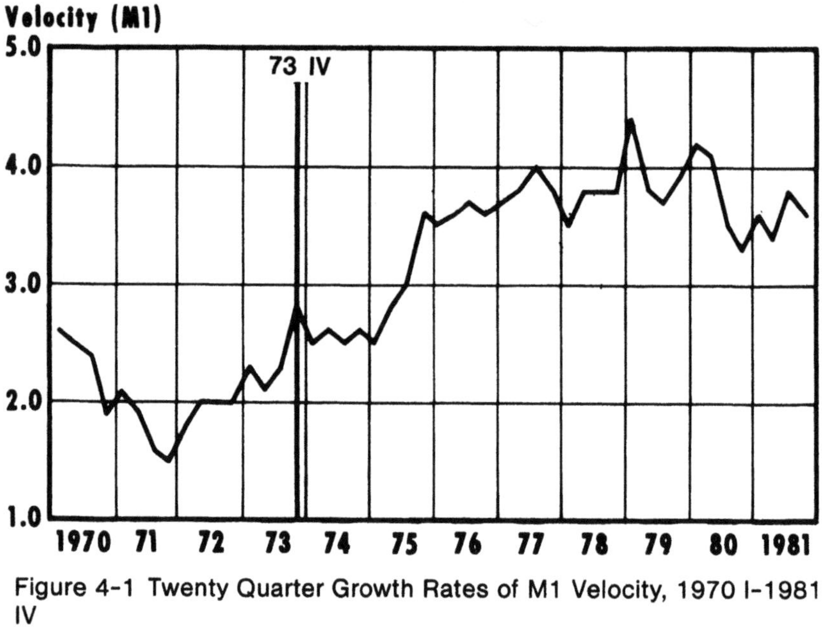

Figure 4-1 Twenty Quarter Growth Rates of M1 Velocity, 1970 I-1981 IV

Table 4-8. Money and Velocity Growth Since 1970: Annual Rate Percent Changes

	M1					*Velocity (M1)*				
From / *To*	*Previous Quarter*	*Two Quarters Ago*	*Four Quarters Ago*	*Eight Quarters Ago*	*Twenty Quarters Ago*	*Previous Quarter*	*Two Quarters Ago*	*Four Quarters Ago*	*Eight Quarters Ago*	*Twenty Quarters Ago*
1970:1	3.9	3.5	3.0	5.4	5.0	0.3	0.0	2.5	2.0	2.6
1970:2	4.2	4.1	3.3	5.0	5.1	1.7	1.0	1.9	1.5	2.5
1970:3	5.0	4.6	4.1	4.7	5.1	2.1	1.9	1.0	1.8	2.4
1970:4	6.4	5.7	4.9	4.4	5.0	−4.0	−1.0	0.0	1.4	1.9
1971:1	7.4	6.9	5.8	4.4	5.1	8.9	2.3	2.1	2.3	2.1
1971:2	9.8	8.6	7.1	5.2	5.3	−1.9	3.4	1.2	1.5	1.9
1971:3	6.5	8.1	7.5	5.8	5.7	0.3	−0.8	0.7	0.8	1.6
1971:4	3.3	4.9	6.7	5.8	5.8	3.9	2.1	2.7	1.3	1.5
1972:1	8.6	5.9	7.0	6.4	6.1	4.9	4.4	1.8	1.9	1.8
1972:2	7.2	7.9	6.4	6.7	6.1	3.2	4.1	3.1	2.1	2.0
1972:3	8.2	7.7	6.8	7.2	6.1	0.3	1.8	3.1	1.9	2.0
1972:4	10.0	9.1	8.5	7.6	6.2	2.8	1.6	2.8	2.8	2.0
1973:1	8.5	9.3	8.5	7.7	6.4	8.1	5.4	3.6	2.7	2.3
1973:2	5.0	6.7	7.9	7.1	6.3	2.6	5.3	3.4	3.2	2.1
1973:3	4.7	4.8	7.0	6.9	6.1	4.6	3.6	4.5	3.8	2.3
1973:4	4.9	4.8	5.8	7.1	5.9	6.9	5.8	5.5	4.2	2.8
1974:1	7.0	5.9	5.4	6.9	5.9	−3.5	1.6	2.6	3.1	2.5
1974:2	3.7	5.4	5.1	6.5	5.9	6.8	1.5	3.6	3.5	2.6
1974:3	3.6	3.7	4.8	5.9	6.0	4.3	5.6	3.6	4.0	2.5
1974:4	4.8	4.2	4.8	5.3	6.1	1.4	2.8	2.2	3.8	2.6
1975:1	3.0	3.9	3.8	4.6	6.1	−1.3	0.0	2.8	2.7	2.5

(*Continued*)

Table 4-8 (*Continued*)

	M1					*Velocity (M1)*				
From / *To*	*Previous Quarter*	*Two Quarters Ago*	*Four Quarters Ago*	*Eight Quarters Ago*	*Twenty Quarters Ago*	*Previous Quarter*	*Two Quarters Ago*	*Four Quarters Ago*	*Eight Quarters Ago*	*Twenty Quarters Ago*
1975:2	6.3	4.6	4.4	4.7	6.2	3.8	1.2	2.0	2.8	2.7
1975:3	7.6	6.9	5.4	5.1	6.3	9.0	6.4	3.2	3.4	3.0
1975:4	3.0	5.3	5.0	4.9	6.1	8.1	8.6	4.8	3.5	3.6
1976:1	5.9	4.4	5.7	4.7	6.1	6.7	7.4	6.9	4.8	3.5
1976:2	6.9	6.4	5.8	5.1	5.9	−0.3	3.1	5.8	3.9	3.6
1976:3	4.3	5.6	5.0	5.2	5.8	2.9	1.3	4.3	3.7	3.7
1976:4	7.7	6.0	6.2	5.6	6.0	2.5	2.7	2.9	3.9	3.6
1977:1	9.8	8.7	7.2	6.4	6.1	5.6	4.1	2.6	4.8	3.7
1977:2	7.4	8.6	7.3	6.6	6.1	4.7	5.2	3.9	4.9	3.8
1977:3	6.9	7.1	7.9	6.5	6.0	5.3	5.0	4.5	4.4	4.0
1977:4	8.7	7.8	8.2	7.2	6.0	−0.6	2.3	3.7	3.3	3.8

1978:1	8.1	8.4	7.8	7.5	5.9	0.9	0.2	2.5	2.6	3.5
1978:2	9.4	8.7	8.3	7.8	6.2	10.2	5.5	3.9	3.9	3.8
1978:3	8.0	8.7	8.5	8.2	6.3	3.7	6.9	3.5	4.0	3.8
1978:4	7.5	7.7	8.2	8.2	6.5	7.7	5.7	5.6	4.6	3.8
1979:1	5.2	6.3	7.5	7.6	6.4	7.1	7.4	7.1	4.8	4.4
1979:2	10.3	7.7	7.7	8.0	6.7	−4.0	1.4	3.5	3.7	3.8
1979:3	9.6	10.0	8.1	8.3	7.0	2.4	−0.9	3.2	3.3	3.7
1979:4	4.6	7.1	7.4	7.8	7.0	4.1	3.2	2.3	3.9	3.9
1980:1	7.0	5.8	7.8	7.7	7.2	5.3	4.7	1.9	4.5	4.2
1980:2	−3.2	1.8	4.4	6.0	6.7	2.2	3.7	3.5	3.5	4.1
1980:3	14.8	5.4	5.6	6.9	7.0	−2.6	−0.3	2.2	2.7	3.5
1980:4	11.6	13.2	7.3	7.4	7.5	3.0	0.1	1.9	2.1	3.3
1981:1	4.6	8.0	6.7	7.3	7.4	13.9	8.3	3.9	2.9	3.6
1981:2	9.6	7.1	10.1	7.2	7.5	−4.5	4.3	2.2	2.8	3.4
1981:3	0.2	4.8	6.4	6.0	7.3	11.2	3.0	5.6	3.9	3.8
1981:4	5.9	3.0	5.0	6.2	7.2	−1.2	4.8	4.5	3.2	3.6
1982:1	10.8	8.3	6.5	6.6	7.3	−10.1	−5.8	−1.5	1.2	2.8

Table 4-9. Velocity Regressions (dependent variable is log (V))

	constant	*T*	*D*	*DT*
60I–73IV	1.27 (292.3)	0.0067 (50.79)		
74I–80IV	1.12 (66.63)	0.0094 (39.83)		
60I–80IV	1.26 (292.26)	0.0074 (84.17)		
	1.26 (261.23)	0.0070 (48.42)	0.022 (2.96)	
	1.27 (270.20)	0.0069 (47.62)		0.00047 (4.51)
	1.27 (326.07)	0.0067 (56.65)	−0.15 (−6.35)	0.0027 (7.48)

corresponds to Hafer and Hein's (1982) distinction between an intercept shift and continuing drift in the money demand equation. The basic equation is

$$\ln V = c_0 + c_1\,T + c_2\,\text{DUMMY} + c_3\,T \cdot \text{DUMMY} \quad (4.11)$$

where DUMMY is defined as in equation 4.8 above and T is a time trend. First we estimate equation 4.11 over the two time periods, 1960I–1973IV and 1974I–1980IV, excluding both dummy variables (see table 4–9). We observe a significant increase in the coefficient on the time trend from 2.68 percent at an annual rate to 3.69 percent. Over the full period, we find that when the level shift and time trend shift dummies are entered separately, they are each significant. When they are entered simultaneously, there is a multicollinearity problem since T-DUMMY is a combination of T and DUMMY. However, both come in significantly, though the shift variable reverses sign.

I conclude from this that the behavior of velocity is consistent with the hypothesized decline in transactions costs and with the observed breakdown in the conventional equation. Monetarism (defined as a faith whose dogma is constant velocity growth) is, apparently, in the eye of the beholder.

Velocity Behavior and Monetary Aggregate Targeting

Hamburger concludes that, since velocity behavior hasn't changed in the post-1973 period, there is no reason to abandon monetary aggregate targeting.

Having established that velocity growth did accelerate in the post-1973 period, I do not accept as an immediate implication that the Federal Reserve should abandon monetary aggregate targeting. Given the alternatives, monetary aggregate targeting still seems the best course; although I question whether targeting assorted and changing money supply definitions is worth the effort involved, compared to directly targeting a reserve aggregate more directly under the Federal Reserve's control.

Monetary policy has been forced to carry the entire burden of anti-inflationary stabilization policy. By maintaining a policy of modest and decelerating monetary growth, the Federal Reserve has accomplished a dramatic decline in inflation. This has, of course, come with a significant real cost in terms of a temporary period of higher unemployment and lower output growth; but this surprised only rational-expectations monetarists, supply siders, and the President.

Monetary aggregate targeting remains a useful strategy for anti-inflationary policy. There is, however, a danger in that financial innovations will, on occasion, alter the degree of restraint desired by the Federal Reserve and intended by its choice of monetary growth targets. It might be useful, therefore, to supplement monetary growth rate targets with a range of real long-term interest rates to protect against both overly stimulative monetary policies when velocity grows unexpectedly rapidly or overly restrictive monetary policy if velocity growth unexpectedly diminishes.

Moving to interest rate targeting instead of monetary aggregate targeting would be dangerous for a couple of reasons. First, it would focus public and political attention on interest rates and make it more difficult to allow interest rates to rise when stabilization objectives require such a movement. Second, in an inflationary environment, we presumably would want to target real rates, and the calculation of real rates may involve even more problems than defining money. Finally, although increased financial instability increases the case for interest rate as opposed to monetary aggregate targeting, it does not guarantee that interest rate targeting now dominates monetary aggregate targeting. That still depends on parameter values and relative size of financial and real disturbances. I haven't seen convincing (or even unconvincing) evidence that suggests increased economic stability would be associated with interest rate targets.

Monetary aggregate targeting continues to have two advantages. First, it is still relatively easy to define an anti-inflationary policy by selecting appropriate monetary growth target ranges. A rate of monetary growth at about the rate of inflation constitutes an approximately neutral policy. Monetary growth rates below the prevailing inflation rate restrain real demand and reduce inflation. Second, the failure of the Federal Reserve to recognize a shift in the trend growth of velocity of 1/2 to 1 percentage point would not have very serious effects on the economy. Given a set of monetary growth targets, the economy would adjust to the new velocity trend at a 1/2 to 1 percentage point change in the inflation rate. Third, maintaining relatively stable monetary growth targets promises at least built-in stability in relation to real sector demand shocks. What real rate constitutes neutral monetary policy? What movement of real rates over the cycle are required to yield the built-in stability associated with a fixed rate of monetary growth over the cycle? And what are the consequences of selecting an inappropriate real rate target? When I become convinced that the Federal Reserve can answer these questions, I will take real interest rate targeting more seriously. Until then, perhaps we should at least not be so committed to the monetarist mythology of stable velocity trends that we fail to recognize that monetary growth targets may need to be adjusted to reflect changes in velocity growth associated with the changing pace of financial innovation.

References

Hafer, R. W., and Scott, E. Hein. "The Shift in Money Demand: What Really Happened?" *Review* Federal Reserve Bank of St. Louis, February 1982.

Hafer, R. W., and Scott E. Hein. "Evidence on the Temporal Stability of the Demand for Money Relationship in the United States." *Review* Federal Reserve Bank of St. Louis, December 1979.

Hamburger, Michael. "Behavior of the Money Stock: Is there a puzzle?" *Journal of Monetary Economics* (1977), 265–288.

Judd, John, and John L. Scadding. "The Search for a Stable Money Demand Function: A Survey of the Post-1973 Literature." *Journal of Economic Literature* (September 1982).

III IMPACT OF INNOVATION ON MONETARY POLICY AND FINANCIAL RISK MANAGEMENT

5 FINANCIAL INNOVATION AND MONETARY POLICY

Jerry L. Jordan

Recent discussions in professional literature and the popular press have focused on the extent to which financial innovation has affected—or in the future might affect—the effectiveness of monetary policy. These discussions have tended to neglect causation in the opposite direction—the extent to which monetary policy actions have been an inducement to the kinds of financial innovations we have observed. Conjectures about financial innovation in the future should be based on some understanding of the forces giving rise to the kinds of innovations that have occurred in the past. A forecast of a specific future innovation may imply a forecast of future inflation, interest rates, or regulatory developments more than it implies a forecast of some technological development.

To the extent that highly inflationary monetary policies in the past (and, therefore, high nominal market interest rates) have spawned certain types of innovations, an environment of less inflation and lower interest rates in the future would not produce the same incentives. Similarly, to the extent past regulatory restrictions on depository institutions spawned certain types of innovations, deregulation or changed regulation of these institutions will change the cost-benefit relationships faced by would-be innovators. The kinds of innovations we are likely to see in the future cannot be assessed except in the context of: (1) the Depository Institutions Deregulation and Monetary Control Act of 1980; (2) a forecast of future legislative and regulatory developments; and (3) a forecast of future inflation and interest rates. The mandated phase-out of Regulation Q interest rate ceilings, the implementation of uniform as well as universal reserve requirements on transactions liabilities at depository institutions and the induced effects of Federal Reserve pricing of services will all affect the kinds of innovation that will occur in the future. And such innovation will be different, or will occur at a different pace, if the rate of inflation and level of interest rates is low, in contrast with the experience of the past few years.

Sweep Accounts and Transactions Deposits

Concerns over the prospects for sweep accounts, especially at the consumer level, involve an implicit forecast about short-term market interest rates. For example, Frank Morris' reluctant conclusion "that we can no longer measure the money supply with any kind of precision" is based on his concern about deposit-sweeping operations [Morris, 1982]. He notes that the practice has been common for large corporate balances for a long time, but recently sweeping has been offered to medium-sized and small businesses. His fear is that sweeping will soon be offered to consumer accounts as well. One rationale he offers for this conjecture is that declining costs of computer terminals will mean the middle-class consumer may have the capability at home of sweeping his account as often as he wishes by activating his bank's computer. Certainly such technological advancements have some influence on innovation in the financial services industry, but the incentive for sweeping of transactions accounts has been more a function of relative yields than of technical feasibility.

Morris cites four factors that contributed to the environment in which recent innovation has occurred: (1) higher interest rates; (2) computer capabilities; (3) prohibition of interest on demand balances; and (4) the structure of noninterest-bearing reserve requirements imposed on some banks. There is little disagreement that such factors contributed to incentives to sweep large corporate balances, and even more recently medium and small business accounts. But the incentives for sweeping of consumer transactions accounts are somewhat different. The first difference, of course, is that payment of interest on consumer transactions accounts is no longer prohibited. With the current ceiling rate at 5.5 percent and such ceilings destined to be phased up and out along with all Regulation Q ceiling rates, the opportunity cost of holding consumer-type transactions deposits is less than business-type demand balances. Morris asserts that "Interest rates are likely to decline in the years ahead.... However, there is no reason to believe that interest rates will fall so low as to eliminate the incentive to shift demand balances to some form of earning asset." I will simply assert the opposite, that there is no reason *not* to believe interest rates will fall enough, so it becomes an empirical issue. How low is low enough? Whatever level of market interest rates is low enough to eliminate the incentive to shift from noninterest-bearing business balances, the level is higher for consumer NOW accounts.

Other questions must be addressed to ascertain what level of market interest rates induces this particular form of disintermediation of consumer accounts to occur. What yield differential compensates for FDIC or FSLIC insurance? What role will minimum balance requirements or other pricing considerations play? How will potential increased use of direct deposit, point-of-sale terminals, automatic teller machines, and debit cards influence the desired average transactions balances of the consumer? A priori, there are as many reasons to believe the consumer will hold larger average transactions balances in depository institutions in the future (relative to his income or wealth) than smaller average balances.

A Framework for Analyzing Financial Innovations and Monetary Policy

We all learned in our first money and banking course that the Federal Reserve had three monetary policy tools. That has been obsolete information for some time, since there is really only one action that our central bank can take to affect overall economic activity. Changes in reserve requirements had not been used for policy purposes even long before the 1980 legislation formally declared that emergency conditions were called for before the Federal Reserve could change reserve requirement ratios for monetary policy purposes. Changes in the discount rate still influence the share of bank reserves that are borrowed from the Federal Reserve, but do not do anything else when policy is focused on a reserve or monetary targeting procedure. That leaves open market operations—monetizing U.S. Government debt—as the only tool available to the central bank.

The simplest world for the monetary policymakers would be one in which there was a direct and predictable relationship between open market operations and economic activity.

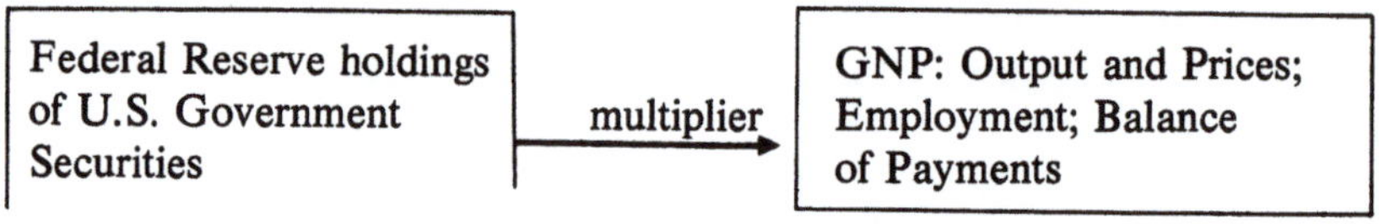

Unfortunately, this multiplier is subject to influence by a great many factors, tends to fluctuate considerably, and cannot be predicted with a high degree of confidence. Consequently, intermediate linkages or indicators of the thrust of monetary policy actions are employed. Financial innovations can and do affect the various linkages, multipliers, or velocities, but whether or not the predictability of the effects of monetary policy actions is influenced is an empirical issue. Innovations resulting from the interactions of market forces tend to be gradual, while innovations in response to changes in regulations or a conflict between barriers caused by regulation and economic incentives, tend to be abrupt. (See figure 5–1.)

By now there is little disagreement among economists that the amount of government debt monetized by the Central Bank has some influence on economic activity. There is still disagreement about the transmission mechanism of such effects, and the timing and quantification of these effects, but at least we agree that open market operations do something. Some of us are persuaded that the growth of the noninterest-bearing debt of the government (possibly relative to the amount of interest-bearing debt) has some significance for analyzing the thrust of Central Bank actions. Some analysts find it useful to separate the total noninterest-bearing debt into its two component uses—bank reserves and currency held by the public—and some find it useful to adjust the actual amount of noninterest-bearing debt of the government to reflect the effects of changes in sterile reserve requirement ratios on the private banking system. Which of these approaches, or some combination of them, improves the monetary authorities' ability to formulate and implement monetary policy is an empirical issue.

Financial innovations are not likely to have effects on the total amount of noninterest-bearing debt of the government, but it has happened on occasion. For example, the creation of the Treasury Note Option in late 1978 changed the behavior of Treasury balances at the Federal Reserve which could have affected the amount of noninterest-bearing debt outstanding in absence of fully offsetting defensive open market operations.

Financial innovations can also affect the ways the banks and the nonbank public hold the government's noninterest-bearing debt. This potential, and the actual experience, have been explored by Allan Meltzer and Jack Tatom (1982).

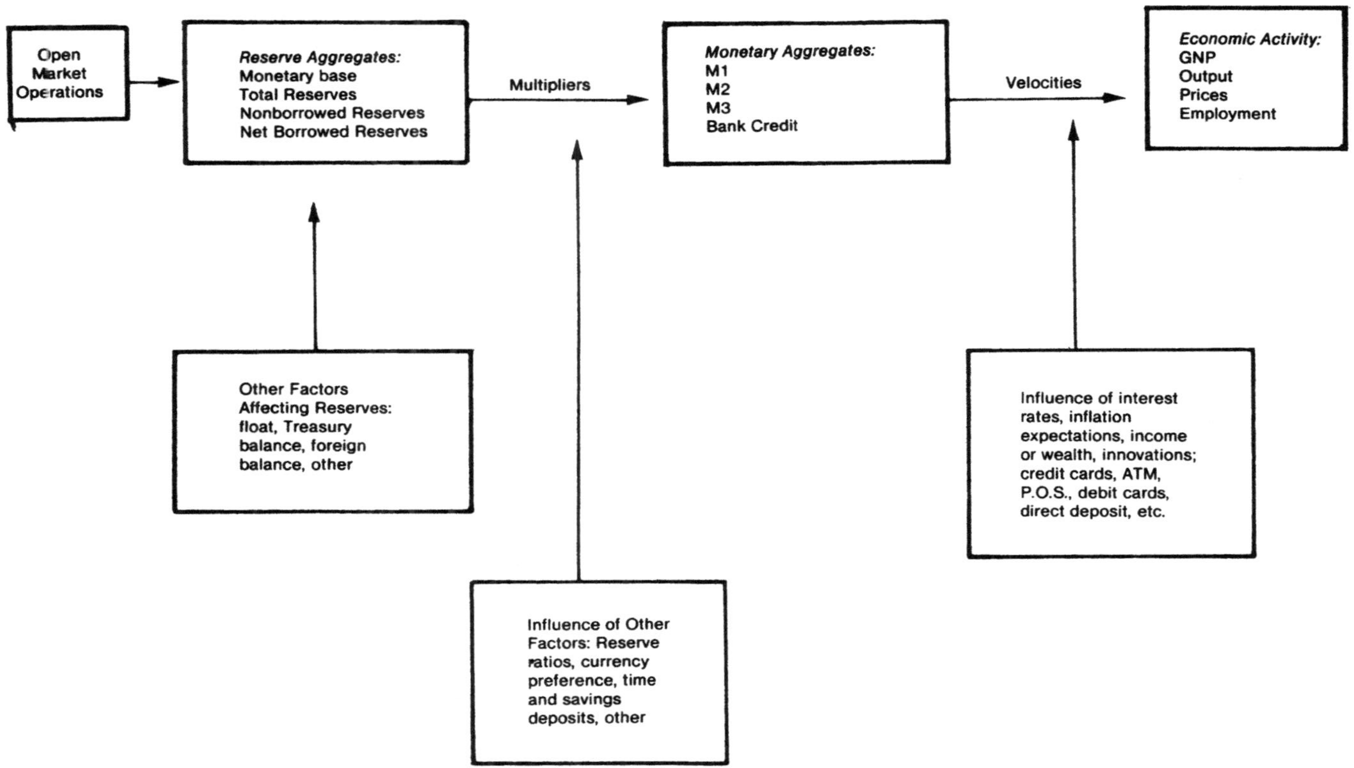

Figure 5-1. Link Between Federal Reserve Monetary Policy and Economic Activity

An alternative approach to analyzing the effects of financial innovations on monetary policy has been to consider whether the amount of money held by the public, for a given amount of noninterest-bearing debt of the government, has been affected. In other words, have the multipliers between the total noninterest-bearing debt, or the bank reserve component of it, and various intermediate monetary aggregates changed as a result of innovations? The framework for analyzing this issue is well known, and Meltzer ( ) has shown how the Brunner-Meltzer money supply model can be used to isolate the potential for innovations to influence the various monetary multipliers. The recent empirical study by Tatom (1982) shows how the creation of Automatic Transfer Service accounts affected some formulations of monetary multipliers, and also reports results for the effects of the introduction of NOW accounts on multipliers.

Factors other than financial innovations also have affected the multipliers over time, occasionally with dramatic effects. The public's willingness to hold cash balances in the form of transactions deposits rather than currency can change for reasons other than innovations. This was shown during the early 1930s or, according to a hypothesis put forth by Weintraub (1980), during the period of credit controls during the spring of 1980. The effective weighted average reserve ratios and the various deposit ratios can change for reasons that are not related to innovations as well as reasons that are. That there is such a potential is not the issue. What is important to the monetary authorities is whether or not such potential can be anticipated in advance or detected sufficiently rapidly after its occurrence to be taken into account by open market operations. Since the elasticities of the various monetary multipliers with respect to the various behavioral and policy parameters are not the same, a change in any parameter, whether related to an innovation or not, will not affect the alternative monetary aggregates in the same way. Consequently, when there are changes in parameters affecting the multipliers, the monetary authorities must decide which of the monetary aggregates is the more reliable indicator of the influence of their actions on economic activity. The empirical evidence available to date is quite clear that a monetary aggregate which includes currency plus all transactions liabilities at depository institutions has been the most reliable indicator of the influence of monetary actions on economic activity. Furthermore, there is no evidence as yet to suggest that either financial innovations or other forces have weakened the capability of the monetary authorities to adequately achieve target growth rates for the narrowly defined money stock.

The issue of which monetary aggregate is the most reliable indicator of the influence of policy actions also has been questioned as a result of concerns over actual or potential financial innovations. Usually the arguments put forth take the form of concerns over problems of identifying and measuring whatever it is that is serving the functions of money or, alternatively, assertions about shifts in the demand for money. Both of these approaches translate into an empirical issue over whether measurable surrogates for the theoretical concept of money are sufficiently reliable so that policymakers can predict the nominal income growth that will be associated with a specified growth of the monetary aggregate. In other words, has the velocity of alternative measures of money been sufficiently predictable over a relevant time span to serve the purposes of policymakers. Numerous recent empirical studies of this issue, including those by Hafer and Hein (1982); and Tatom (1982), Ott (1982), and Hein (1982), respectively, in February, April, May and June/July issues of the St. Louis Federal Reserve Bank's *Review*, have concluded that so far nothing has happened—either as a result of financial innovations or for other reasons—that reduces the reliability of the narrowly defined money stock as an indicator.

Recent Experience—1980–1982

The behavior of monetary aggregates and various interpretations that have been offered illustrate the danger of prematurely concluding that anything unusual has happened to the demand for money. In March of 1980, the Federal Reserve imposed pervasive credit controls for the first, only, and last time under authority of the 1969 legislation. During the second quarter of 1980, the level of M1 declined, but nominal GNP declined by more, so the ratio GNP/M1 also declined. The observation that M1 declined caused some analysts to conclude that the demand for M1 declined (while interest rates also declined sharply), but the observed decline of velocity could easily have been interpreted to mean the demand for M1 actually increased (or declined less than the money supply). The St. Louis Federal Reserve economists mentioned above have thoroughly analyzed this period and conclude, along with Weintraub and others, that the behavior of the money stock during that period can best be explained by factors on the supply side rather than the demand side.

During the first quarter of 1981, it was observed that nominal income rose much more rapidly than M1, so the ratio of the two, or velocity, rose. A common interpretation was that the demand for money had declined, possibly because of increased use of money market fund balances as an abode of purchasing power. How the decline of velocity in the second quarter of 1980 and the rise of velocity in the first quarter of 1981 could both be taken as evidence of a decrease in the demand for money balances was never explained.

For those who accept simple answers that serve to adequately explain events rather than more complex and apparently sophisticated explanations, the rapid growth in nominal income in the first quarter of 1981 appeared to reflect nothing more than the lagged effects of rapid money growth in the prior two quarters. Money growth slowed sharply in early 1981, but GNP growth did not (because of the lags), so the ratio went up. At the time, it seemed that the best assumption to make, based on long and consistent historical experience, was that if the slower money growth were maintained at a steady rate, nominal income growth would also slow to a point where the historical velocity trend was reestablished. And, of course, that is what actually happened.

Analysis of that period was unusually confusing because of the Federal Reserve's emphasis on M1A, M1B, and M1B-adjusted. Some of the rhetoric of the period implied that the demand for M1B should have gone up (velocity down) because of the introduction of nationwide NOW accounts. The observation that the velocity of money appeared to rise while the demand for that form of money was assumed to be rising gave some analysts a reason for caution in drawing conclusions, but it probably didn't bother as many observers as it should have. As Tatom (1982), Ott (1982), and Hein (1982) have all concluded, by the end of the year it did not appear that much of anything had happened to the demand for (velocity of) M1B, either as a result of NOW accounts, money market fund balances, or anything else.

Thus far, 1982 has been a mirror image of 1981. During the first quarter of 1982, money growth (M1B) was very rapid while nominal income growth was not, so the ratio of income to money fell. The simple explanation is that the decline of income growth was the lagged effect of the earlier sharp decline in money growth, while the coincident sharp acceleration in money growth would not be expected to affect income until later in the year. Consequently, the apparent drop in velocity in the first quarter was likely to be offset by a corresponding rise later, and, on balance, the historic trend would be maintained.

For those who like complicated explanations, once again conjectures about shifts in the demand for money emerged. In contrast to 1981, the early 1982 shift was supposed to have been upward and the reason given was that sometime between Thanksgiving and Valentine's Day people decide to hold more cash balances, both in the form of currency and NOW balances. The simultaneous sharp rise in market interest rates and extremely rapid growth of the money stock was interpreted to mean that even a 15 percent rate of increase of M1 from October 1981 to January 1982 was restrictive because, it was asserted, demand was increasing even more rapidly than supply. This, presumably, was the opposite of what happened in the spring of 1980, when both the money stock and interest rates fell sharply.

In 1981, it was argued that more attention should be paid to more inclusive measures of money, or even some measure of the amount of credit, because of declining relative importance of M1-type money. But by early 1982, the argument was that the public's increased preference for M1-type money meant that its rapid growth was not a reliable indicator of monetary stimulus.

What has remained consistent over at least the past fifteen years is the basic nature of the ad hoc explanations for why accelerations in money growth are not expansionary and decelerations or declines are not contractionary. In the 1960s, the assertion was that faster money growth merely reflected the fact that the economy's transactions needs for cash were rising because of faster nominal income growth. In the early and mid-1970s, the more familiar assertion was that faster money growth was not really stimulative after taking account of the faster inflation. At various times, the growth of Eurodollar deposits, the transactions of Edge Act corporations, the increased use of repurchase agreements, the increased use of credit cards, the behavior of Treasury tax and loan accounts, and electronic funds transfers systems have been alluded to as reasons for concerns about the effectiveness or reliability of monetary policy. Whenever the explanation given for faster or slower growth in an aggregate is that the demand for it has increased or decreased, you can be certain that an interpretation of expansionary or contractionary implications is being ruled out.

What has been unusual about the past few years is the frequency of assertions that money demand has shifted. That no doubt reflects the apparent increase in the short-run volatility of money growth for which the policymakers do not wish to be blamed. Blaming the fickle money holder seems to be attractive, but I doubt it is any more convincing than blaming inflation on greed and unemployment on callousness.

Figure 5–2 summarizes the assertions and accompanying developments of the past few years. As Scott Hein (1982) points out, if money demand shifted down in Q 2/80, then it must have shifted back up in the second half. Similarly, if money demand shifted down in Q 1/81, then it must have shifted back up in Q 2/81, when income growth and velocity fell while money growth accelerated. But, then it must have shifted back down in Q 3/81 when income growth and velocity rose, but money did not (although interest rates fell?), before it is asserted to have shifted up again in Q 1/82. In Q 3/82, income growth was more rapid than money growth (velocity rose again while interest rates fell) so a downward shift in money demand offsetting the

Date	Assertion	Actual $\dot{M}$	Actual $\dot{Y}$	Actual $\dot{V}$	i
Q 2/80	Decr. M^d	Down	Down	Down	Down
Q 1/81	Decr. M^d	Down	Up	Up	Down
Q 1/82	Incr. M^d	Up	Down	Down	Up

Figure 5-2. Effect of Change in Money Demand on Selected Macroeconomic Variables

upward shift in Q 1/82 will no doubt be given as the explanation for observed developments. But if every apparent shift is matched by an apparent opposite shift within the subsequent two quarters, how useful is it to policymakers or to the public to employ such arguments?

Nominal Income as a Goal of Monetary Policy

Periodically, someone suggests that the growth of nominal GNP should be the goal of monetary policy. My reaction is always the same; namely, "Of course! What else would it be?" When present or former officials of the Federal Reserve suggest that it would be a change in approach for the FOMC to have a goal expressed in terms of the growth of nominal income, then I wonder what it is they think they have been doing. Targeting some growth range of monetary aggregates was never an end in itself, any more than targeting some level of interest rates was an end in itself (although, quite clearly, there have been periods when the FOMC did try to set the level of nominal interest rates as though it were a final objective).

In his AEA Presidential Address in 1967, Milton Friedman went to some length to explain that monetary policy actions affect nominal magnitudes. Whether one is talking about the effects of open market operations in terms of bank reserves, the monetary base, monetary aggregates, or market interest rates, these are all nominal magnitudes and, at least theoretically, can be related to nominal income.

The recent "Proposal for Change" offered by Frank Morris (1982) is, in part, puzzling, and, in part, shocking. First, he suggests that the goal of monetary policy would be stated as the rate of growth of total liquid assets, total debt of the nonfinancial sector, or the nominal GNP. Then, he tells us that the goal rate of growth of the chosen variable would be one which would be compatible with a continued deceleration of the inflation rate. That sounds good, but he doesn't tell us how to relate total liquid assets or total debt of the nonfinancial sector to the inflation rate. Instead, he tells us these would be good goals because they have a stable relationship to nominal GNP. That makes his use of the expression *goal for policy* somewhat confusing. If the criterion for choosing a target or indicator for use by the FOMC is that variable which has the closest relationship to nominal income, then what else is it the FOMC is trying to do if it is not to influence the growth of nominal GNP?

Morris (1983) goes on to tell us that "Control theory would suggest that the nominal GNP should be the preferred goal. One advantage of the nominal GNP as a goal is that it would upgrade the quality of the dialogue on monetary policy. There would be much more substance in such a dialogue than the current one over an M-1, the meaning of which is growing increasingly obscure". That is a very interesting admission. If the current FOMC dialogue over targets for M1 growth are not in the context of the expected nominal GNP growth, then what are they doing? Does the FOMC view the growth of monetary aggregates as a final objective? I doubt it. When the chairman of the Federal Reserve Board testifies that the monetary growth targets of the FOMC are consistent with Administration objectives for economic activity, he is saying that the targeted growth ranges of the monetary aggregates are expected to be accompanied by growth of nominal income within a specified range.

But, Morris (1982) tells us there are problems with having nominal GNP as the goal. One problem, he says, is that it may be more difficult for the FOMC to obtain a consensus on a nominal GNP goal than it would be to obtain a consensus on total liquid assets. I don't understand that. If the reason for setting an objective in terms of the growth of total liquid assets is its "very stable and predictable" relationship to GNP, how do you choose a desired growth range for liquid assets if you cannot agree on the desired growth of GNP? How can there be a dialogue about whether a certain growth rate is too fast, too slow, or just right except in terms of the expected growth of GNP?

"In addition," Morris (1982) argues, "problems may arise in reconciling the FOMC's GNP goal and the Administration's GNP objective." That is an incredible admission. Either the FOMC's monetary policy objectives are consistent with the Administration's objectives for economic activity, or they are not. Twice each year, the chairman of the FOMC must appear before Congress to explain the Federal Reserve's policies and indicate whether or not the policies are consistent with Administration's goals. The suggestion that the FOMC should not express their goals for economic activity in terms of nominal GNP because it would then be obvious that their monetary policies are not consistent with the Administration's objectives is unacceptable. It may be appropriate for the FOMC to have goals for the growth of nominal GNP that are different from the Administration's. But it is not appropriate to deliberately obscure that fact, especially when Congress requires the Federal Reserve to testify on that important issue.

One more point on Morris' "Proposal for Change." He offers an example of his preferred approach by saying, "Let us assume that the FOMC's goal is a 10 percent growth in total liquid assets *and that a 5 percent growth in total bank reserves would be expected to be associated with that goal*" [emphasis added]. How was a 5 percent growth of reserves arrived at? Where is the analytical framework (and supporting empirical evidence) relating bank reserves and total liquid assets? How reliable is this linkage? There are mountains of evidence bearing on the relationships between various reserve aggregates and various monetary aggregates. Is the relationship between total bank reserves and total liquid assets more stable and predictable? Until such evidence is forthcoming, the possibility of this alternative transmission mechanism providing a more reliable total throughput relationship between open market operations and nominal GNP growth will have to remain an unsupported conjecture.

The Reagan Administration, Monetary Control, and Targeting Nominal GNP

In February 1981, the new Administration stated a long-run objective of reducing monetary growth in order to reduce inflation. Specifically, compared to the actual growth of money that occurred in 1980, the Administration assumes a gradual but steady reduction in the growth of money to one-half that rate by 1986 [Annual Report of the Council of Economic Advisers, 1982]. The chairman of the Board of Governors of the Federal Reserve System has publically endorsed that objective on several occasions. It is hard to know what conclusion to draw when other Federal Reserve officials indicate they do not even know what money is, let alone how to control it.

The Full Employment and Balanced Growth Act of 1978 requires that the Administration set annual numerical goals for key indicators over a five-year horizon leading toward a group of interim goals set forth by the Congress [Annual Report of the Council of Economic Advisers, 1982]. The interim goal for inflation is 3 percent, and the ultimate goal is zero. The current Administration fully supports these Congressionally mandated goals, and presumably the Federal Reserve does also. Reducing inflation to 3 percent and then to zero means reducing nominal GNP growth to a rate consistent with a 3 percent inflation, and then with a zero rate of inflation. Since inflation is the word we use for erosion of the purchasing power of money, it seems pretty clear that we have a long-term objective of stopping the erosion of the purchasing power of money. If we are going to succeed, we better have some ideas about what money is and how to stabilize its purchasing power.

The Reagan Administration states that, "Inflation is essentially a monetary phenomenon" and "A decrease in money growth is the necessary strategy to end inflation" [Annual Report of the Council of Economic Advisers, 1982]. The Administration argues that "the monetary aggregate that is selected for policy purposes should be chosen with two factors in mind. One is that growth of the aggregate should be closely related to a primary objective of policy, which is to reduce inflation. This means that the aggregate must be closely related to national income in current prices. The second factor is that the Federal Reserve should be able to control the aggregate." Furthermore, "The Federal Reserve has the ability to control the M1 aggregate with a reasonable degree of precision" [Annual Report of the Council of Economic Advisers, 1982].

The *Annual Report of the Council of Economic Advisers* (1982) goes on to state that "Financial innovations in recent years have complicated the evaluation of the inflationary potential of monetary growth. The development of new financial instruments necessitated a recent redefinition of the monetary aggregates used by the Federal Reserve. The new measure of transactions balances (M1), in addition to including the public's holdings of currency and demand deposits at commercial banks, also includes the new types of checkable deposits offered by financial institutions, such as negotiable orders of withdrawal (NOW) accounts." Further improvement in the ability of the central bank to achieve target growth rates of the money supply can and are being made, and the Administration has endorsed the steps that the Federal Reserve is voluntarily taking, in addition to the steps mandated by the Depository Institutions Deregulation and Monetary Control Act of 1980, to simplify the structure of reserve requirements.

> In a discussion of monetary rules, the Council states that "One of the Administration's long-run objectives is the elimination of inflation. The implementation of a monetary policy that is consistent with this objective can be viewed in the following way. Each year, the monetary authorities would announce the rate of growth of the money supply that is consistent with achieving their medium-term objective for nominal income and inflation. Over the longer run, the rate of growth of the money supply must be consistent with the achievement of the rate of nominal income implied by the inflation objective. To implement this procedure,

the Federal Reserve would determine the rate of growth of total bank reserves that is consistent with the targeted growth of the deposit component of M1. Open market operations of the Federal Reserve would expand the monetary base by a sufficient amount to provide total bank reserves and the currency component of targeted M1 growth."

"Ultimately, the Federal Reserve would set a reserve growth path consistent with the desired price level performance on the basis of the estimates of several parameters. These would include the trend path of real output, the trend of M1 velocity, and the trend of the ratio of M1 to the monetary base. As these changed, the targets for nominal income, M1 growth, and the growth of the monetary base would be altered to maintain a stable price level. Unexpected changes in any of these parameters could be offset to maintain long-run price stability" [Annual Report of the Council of Economic Advisers, 1982].

An illustration of how this approach might be applied in practice follows. Given a five-year interim target, the goal for inflation in 1987 would be 3 percent, consistent with the mandate of the 1978 legislation. Assuming that the long-run potential growth of real output in the economy is somewhere between 3 and 4 percent (depending on the growth of the labor force and productivity), a nominal GNP growth of 6 to 7 percent in 1987 is implied. Table 5–1 illustrates how the goals for nominal income and inflation would be related to targets for monetary growth based on the historical relationship between nominal GNP and M1.

The projected split between real output and prices is arbitrarily half and half and ignores the cross-product term. The objective is not to forecast the division of nominal income into its price and output components, but rather to produce a sustained decline in the rate of growth of nominal income until it is consistent with the inflation objective. For the first year or two, it is quite possible that the growth of output will be more and therefore prices less, or the rate of inflation will be higher while output growth is lower for a given

Table 5-1. Illustration of 5-Year Goals (percentage changes, Q4 to Q4)

	*1982**	*1983*	*1984*	*1985*	*1986*	*1987*
Nominal GNP	7.5	9.0	8.2	7.4	6.8	6.0
Real Output	1.5	4.5	4.1	3.7	3.4	3.0
Prices	6.0	4.5	4.1	3.7	3.4	3.0
M1	5.5	5.0	4.5	4.0	3.5	3.0
Velocity	2.0	4.0	3.7	3.4	3.3	3.0

*Projected

nominal income. Many factors, including fiscal policy developments, international developments, and regulatory policy, will affect the actual rate of inflation and growth of real output, but the objective for the longer-run monetary policy strategy should be to produce a steady deceleration of monetary growth that is consistent with the longer-run nominal income and inflation growth objectives. This illustration indicates that the long-run trend growth of the income velocity of money of about 3 percent is expected to be maintained over this time horizon. Also, the growth of M1 in 1986 (3.5%) is consistent with the Administration's stated objective of cutting money growth in half from 1980 to 1986.

Conclusions

The considerable amount of discussion in the past few years about the effects of financial innovations on the formulation and/or implementation of monetary policy actions has not produced any new ideas nor any new empirical results. The policymakers continue to find it useful to employ a reserve aggregate operating target in the short-run implementation of policy, and the narrowly defined money stock (M1) is still the most reliable indicator of the influence of policy actions on economic activity. The relative merits of alternative reserve aggregates, such as nonborrowed reserves, total reserves, or the monetary base, may be influenced by regulatory actions or by such institutional changes as the return to contemporaneous reserve accounting. However, financial innovations have not made the concept obsolete.

Similarly, the empirical definition of transactions-type money (M1) has been influenced by developments such as the introduction of NOW accounts. However, the usefulness of such an intermediate aggregate to serve as an indicator of the thrust of policy actions has not been undermined.

The argument that policymakers should establish long-run objectives in terms of the growth of nominal income (GNP) is part of the strategy of gradually reducing the growth of the money stock over a period of several years. One-year targets for monetary growth are not essential for successful implementation of the strategy, but a multiyear objective of achieving a steady, noninflationary rate of monetary growth is necessary. Whether one-year targets are best expressed in terms of the monetary base or transactions money (M1) is partly an empirical issue and partly dependent on the credibility of the monetary authorities. The extent to which short-run deviations of monetary growth (under one year) can be tolerated by the monetary authorities is also a function of their credibility. Emphasizing broader measures of money or credit, or total liquid assets, which are not subject to close control by the monetary policymakers would not enhance their credibility. And that is still the number one long-run monetary policy issue—do people really believe our central bank is both able and willing to control inflation over time?

References

1. *Annual Report of the Council of Economic Advisers, 1982.*
2. Hafer, R. W. and Scott E. Hein. "The Shift in Money Demand: What Really Happened?" *Review*, Federal Reserve Bank of St. Louis (February 1982), 15–16.
3. Hein, Scott E. "Short-Run Money Growth Velocity: Evidence of Misbehaving Money Demand?" *Review*, Federal Reserve Bank of St. Louis (June 1982), 35–36.
4. Meltzer, A. H. "The Effects of Financial Innovation on the Instruments of Monetary Policy."
5. Morris, Frank E. "Do the Monetary Aggregates Have a Future as Targets of Federal Reserve Policy?" *New England Economic Review* (March/April 1982), 5–10.
6. Ott, Mack. "Money, Credit and Velocity." *Review*, Federal Reserve Bank of St. Louis (May 1982), 33–34.
7. Tatom, John A. "Recent Financial Innovations: Have They Distorted the Meaning of M1?" *Review*, Federal Reserve Bank of St. Louis (April 1982), 23–32.
8. Weintraub, Robert. "The Impact of the Federal Reserve System's Monetary Policies on the Nation's Economy (Second Report)." Staff Report of the Subcommittee on Domestic Monetary Policy, House Committee on Banking, Finance and Urban Affairs, 96 Congress, 2 Session (GPO, 1980), 17.

6 FINANCIAL INNOVATIONS IN THE 1980s

J. Richard Zecher

Economic theory does not have a very satisfying story to tell about major innovation—the kind of innovation that dramatically changes resource allocation, the menu and price of goods and services available, the role of government, and the structure of markets. A historical fact is that such innovations tend to occur in waves that extend over decades. After the fact, the origins of these waves may be traceable to, for example, enclosures, steam power, the internal combustion engine, or the transistor.

Such major innovations change the opportunities available to investors. As a practical matter, these changes manifest themselves as changes in relative prices and perceived rates of return and/or risk. Economic theory offers a more adequate analytical framework to understanding changed investment decisions, production patterns, consumption patterns, and the response of government to what may be a radically changed set of economic interests of individuals and groups in the economy.

The current period in the financial markets can only be described as one of substantial innovation. Major resource shifts in every part of the financial system have occurred and continue to occur. Traditional financial firms are offering a much wider range of services that greatly reduce the cost of managing financial returns and risks. Whole new industries specializing in the transfer of financial risk have grown up and are reaching maturity. At the same time, financial markets have become totally global in nature, antiquating notions of purely national money and credit markets and confronting businesses and governments with a completely new set of opportunities and constraints. Old methods of financial management and of financial regulation are largely irrelevant or harmful in this environment.

While the economics of innovation may remain an underdeveloped area, economic theory does have much to offer in understanding parts of the innovative process once it is begun. It is to these areas that attention is turned in this paper.

The Nature of Innovation

From the viewpoint of a private firm, questions about financial innovation can be divided into three parts. The first deals with the sources of innovation; can they be identified, understood, predicted, and affected or controlled? The second deals with how the marketplace signals that innovations have (or will) occur: these questions relate to how relative prices, rates of return, and risk are affected by a financial innovation. In general, innovation will alter or destroy some profitable opportunities and create some new ones, and these changes are transmitted ultimately through price-return-risk market signals. Finally, a third set of questions deal with the appropriate business response to market (price-return-risk) signals resulting from an innovation: which lines of business should be reduced, altered or eliminated, which begun or expanded.

The past fifteen years have seen a well above average amount of financial innovations arising from a variety of sources. The resulting change in market signals and opportunities—reflected primarily in changed relative prices-return-and risks—have wrought major upheavals in the way banks and other financial firms do business.

The Changed Monetary Regime

The process of change or innovation is continual and, in some fundamental sense, all parts of the economic and political system affects and are affected by this process. Yet to analyze some part of it, say the role of financial firms, it is necessary to break into the process somewhere, to identify a set of initial changes that set in motion further changes.

One major change that has been occurring over the past 15 to 20 years is a complete revamping of the U.S. and world monetary regimes. An early hint of this change was the movement in U.S. monetary policy in the late 1960s to a more inflationary posture. Stronger evidence was provided in 1968, when the U.S. severed the link between the dollar and gold, reneging on the $35 per ounce price guaranteed to foreign central banks that had been the keystone of the Bretton Woods Agreement. Finally, in August 1971, the dollar was more or less floated on international exchanges, and monetary authorities around the world found their money-creation policies much less constrained—or at least constrained differently—by balance of payments/exchange rate considerations.

In the United States, this newfound monetary freedom ushered in an era of more rapid, and occasionally explosive, monetary growth rates. At the same time, and perhaps of more significance to financial innovation, monetary growth became much more variable, with periods of rapid growth alternating with periods of slow growth.

Figure 6–1 displays the rapid and generally accelerating U.S. money growth during the 1970s as measured by two-year average growth rates. The longer-run growth path of money has been generally rising over the past two decades. Although not shown in figure 6–1, two-year average inflation rates have generally risen over this period and have also mirrored the rises and falls in money growth—usually with about a two-year lag. Inflation has also been more volatile than money growth, in particular rising above money growth rates in the late 1970s and falling below money growth in 1982 (and 1983?). Figure 6–1 also shows the uptrend in short-run money growth volatility, calculated as the variance of monthly growth rates around a one-year moving average growth rate. In general, these two changes signify a change in monetary regime from one of low and stable money growth to one of higher and more variable growth.

As several other papers prepared for this conference are addressed to this changed monetary regime, I will simply list here some conclusions I have drawn from U.S. monetary experience in the period covered in figure 6–1.

Long-Run Money Growth and Inflation. The period covered in figure 6–1 seems to me quite consistent with the historical relationship between longer-run money growth and inflation—accelerating money growth in the 1970s was accompanied by accelerating inflation, and the opposite since 1979.

Inflation Dynamics. The fact that inflation rose faster than money growth rose in the 1970s and has fallen faster than money growth fell since then is

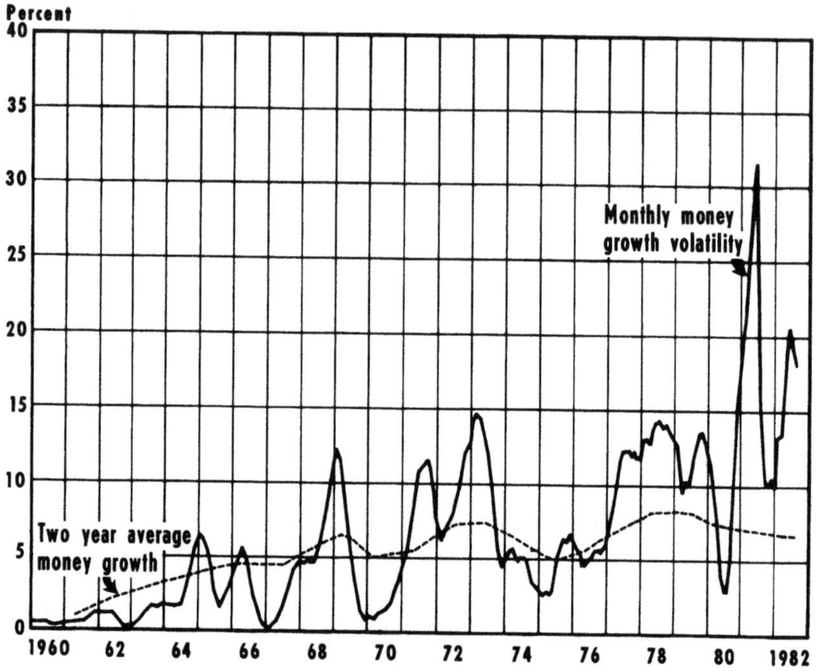

Figure 6-1 Money Growth and Volatility.

also consistent with traditional theories that emphasize conservation of money balances as inflation and interest rates rise, and the converse. In particular, expenditures (and inflation) rose relative to money balances in the late 1970s as interest rates rose sharply, and the opposite has occurred in the 1980s.

Money Growth and Output. Money growth rates have continued to be highly procyclical in this period, generally rising during economic expansions and falling during contractions.

Short-Run Volatility of Money Growth. The greatly increased short-run (monthly) volatility of money growth may be somewhat unsettling in any case to financial and other markets, although it is difficult to maintain this view unadorned in light of the short-run monetary experiences in certain other economies, e.g., Germany and Switzerland. It may be that short-run money growth volatility is most unsettling to markets in a context where there is no believable policy commitment to either stable or low inflation or to countercyclical monetary policy. In such a context, the high money growth volatility of recent years can introduce rapidly changing anticipations of inflation, economic activity, and of the future course of monetary policy itself.

The change in monetary regime characterized by these conclusions is not the only set of initial changes that have set in motion the highly innovative period in the financial markets that we are now witnessing, but I believe it is the most important of these changes.

Other initial changes, such as changed regulation or the development of powerful and inexpensive computing capabilities, can also be cited. But even here, the direction and timing of technological innovation in financial markets is strongly conditioned by other changes that are more directly related to the new monetary regime. For example, higher and more variable inflation and interest rates have provided important inducements to manage risk better in traditional ways—by diversifying product lines, customer groups, and expanding into international markets—and in nontraditional ways—by using highly specialized risk-management techniques, including financial futures and options. These market responses have conditioned the pace and direction of technological innovation and have placed great stress on the regulatory structure.

Accelerating inflation during most of the 1970s and decelerating inflation more recently have provided a lot of new information for investors to digest. Notions about how to hedge against or benefit from rising and falling inflation now have to be confronted with the type of information shown in table 6–1. Rates of return on various real and financial assets would appear to be highly sensitive to rising and falling inflation, but not always in ways we were taught to expect. This is one rough measure of the changed risk/return trade-off in the marketplace that is more closely related to significant longer-run changes in the inflation rate.

Another rough measure of changed risk/return trade-offs under the new regime relates to its short-run volatility. In figure 6–2, the monthly variance of 3-month Treasury bill returns (around a yearly moving average) are shown for the period 1960 to 1982. This substantially increased volatility in financial markets has made it both more difficult and more important to assess and manage financial risk.

A third broad measure of the changed financial environment is represented by the increased financial risk of international transactions resulting from large fluctuations in currency exchange rates. As with interest rate volatility, exchange rate volatility has greatly increased the importance of better managing the foreign exchange exposure of international transactions.

Table 6-1. Returns to Assets Shift as Inflation Slows (compound annual percentage change, adjusted for inflation)

	Year-end 1969 to year-end 1979	*Year-end 1979 to June 1982*
Gold[1]	20.8	−20.3
Housing[2]	2.5	−0.6
Bonds[3]	−0.2	3.1
Money market instruments[4]	−0.5	4.7

[1]London afternoon fixing, average of daily figures.

[2]Median price, existing homes.

[3]20-year corporate AAA bonds, with reinvestment of coupon payments at commercial-paper rate.

[4]Prime 4–6 month commercial paper.

Data: International Monetary Fund, National Association of Realtors, Federal Reserve; and Chase estimates for June 1982.

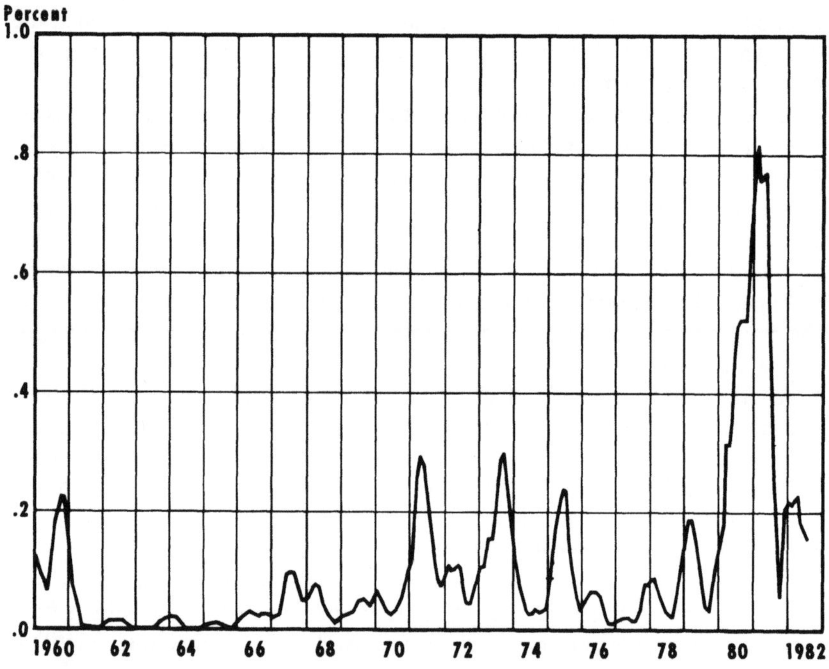

Figure 6-2 Volatility in Interest Rates (Variance/Mean for Previous 12 Months in 90-Day T-Bill Rates).

The massive wealth redistribution implicit in the data of table 6–1 and the increased short-run volatility in domestic and international financial markets shown in figure 6–2 have greatly expanded the resources devoted to financial risk management. Whole new industries, offering financial futures and options services, have grown up over this period. Moreover, these changes have raised profound questions about the ability of our political process to provide a stable economic environment in terms of inflation and growth.

Several unintended results of our high inflation, financially volatile environment include:

(1) obsolescence of much of the regulatory structure surrounding banks and savings institutions, particularly regulation relating to maximum interest rates, geographic limitations on competitors, and limits on products and services that regulated firms can provide
(2) changed management techniques in financial institutions that respond to the more dangerous environment by diversification—geographically and internationally in terms of assets and liabilities—and maturity matching and the use of futures and options in terms of the residual interest rate risk.

In a sense, the regulatory and private management systems are responding to the same changed economic environment (and to each other), but the process of change in the private and public sectors is quite different.

Regulatory Change

One view of economic regulation is that it is designed to reverse alleged market failures that lead to excessively high prices due to monopoly power or to obviate other undesirable results, such as the production of too much pollution, fraud, etc. In this view, regulators protect weaker members of society from their stronger brethren, improve resource allocation over what a free market would yield, and do all this at a cost that is in line on the margin with the benefits derived.

Another, admittedly more cynical, view is that regulation reflects the outcome of competition among groups for scarce resources. This view is based on the plain truth that every regulation reallocates resources: some groups are benefited and some are taxed. Competition in the political arena results in a regulatory structure that reflects the relative effective strength of the competing groups. In general, victory belongs to the relatively small and well-organized group that has a high per capital stake in the outcome. The resulting regulatory structure will improve economic performance only by accident, but it will reflect a type of economic/political equilibrium that is stable until something happens to change the size of the wealth transfer or the relative economic interests and strength of the paying or benefiting groups.

The second view of regulation provides insight into a major regulatory change in financial markets—the unfixing of commission rates on the New York Stock Exchange. This episode, I believe, is also instructive for the current state of disarray in our overall financial regulatory structure.

Each year prior to 1975, there was in place a fixed commission rate schedule for all trades on the New York Stock Exchange. This schedule was set by the NYSE, changed from time to time, and sanctioned by the Securities and Exchange Commission. Since the schedule was a NYSE rule approved by the SEC, the enforcement power of the federal government was fully behind the fixed commission rate structure.

After 1975, all public transactions were determined by unfettered price competition among brokers. The competitive rate structure after 1975 can be used to estimate, after adjustment for inflation and other factors, what the competitive rate structure would have been in earlier years. Comparing the fixed rate with the estimated competitive rate for various size trades that actually occurred in the years 1960 to 1975, for both individuals and institutions, then provides a measure of how much customers were overcharged (or undercharged). The total amount of overcharging (or undercharging) is a measure of the wealth transferred by this price-fixing regulation. Admittedly, this is a maximum estimate of the regulatory wealth transfer or tax, because much of the overcharging or undercharging was reduced by varying service levels. For example, very small transactions received lowered service levels, while very large transactions, which paid much more than the competitive brokerage fee, were given many extra services. Thus, nonprice competition mitigated the size of the regulatory tax, but probably didn't eliminate it.

In table 6–2, estimates of the maximum amount of overcharging or wealth transfer are provided for the years 1960 to 1976. The next-to-last column shows that the estimated overcharges rose in the aggregate from over $90 million in 1960 to just under $400 million in 1968, the year that the Justice Department became interested in the anticompetitive nature of fixed commission and the year that fixed commission began to be removed piecemeal. Tax rates, the proportion of total commission that represent overcharges, also peaked in 1967–68, as can be seen in the final column of table 6–2.

Our interpretation of these events is that the fixed commission structure survived from the 1790s to 1960 in a kind of regulatory equilibrium, not

Table 6-2. Net Regulatory Tax as a Percent of Commissions Paid on the New York Stock Exchange

	Total Commissions	*Net Tax*	*Percentage Net Tax*
1960	$220,958	$ 90,360	0.41
1961	302,928	127,378	0.42
1962	276,578	115,251	0.42
1963	312,620	129,117	0.41
1964	353,424	153,675	0.43
1965	444,832	202,300	0.45
1966	518,873	243,739	0.47
1967	686,709	333,357	0.49
1968[a]	827,776	394,750	0.48
1969	577,867	205,464	0.36
1970	659,912	274,556	0.42
1971[b]	835,286	346,387	0.41
1972[c]	808,011	291,242	0.36
1973[d]	771,799	250,149	0.32
1974	738,641	250,225	0.34
1975[e]	1,038,760	274,157	0.26
1976	974,656	157,455	0.16

[a]December 5, 1968, new schedule for 1,000 shares or more.
[b]April 5, 1971, surcharge on orders of 1,000 shares or less.
[c]March 24, 1972, new overall rate structure.
[d]September 25, 1973, 10 percent increase for orders $5,000 or less; 15 percent increase for orders $5,000.01 to $300,000.
[e]May 1, 1975, all rates negotiable.

taxing enough to generate really strong opposition to fixed rates. During the 1960s, primarily as a result of average trade size increases for both individuals and for institutions, the tax rate and the amount taxed both rose sharply. This occurred because there are strong economies of size in brokerage, so larger trades were taxed much more heavily. The opposition to fixed commissions rose with the tax rate and the amount taxed; and, despite several attempts to salvage the system by lowering fixed commission—especially for the more heavily taxed traders of large blocks of stock, the system was made fully price competitive by 1976.

To take one major banking regulation by way of analogy, Regulation Q interest rate ceilings have experienced a similar history in recent years, although the elimination of these ceilings unfortunately is still just around the corner. In table 6–3, the last two columns show the Regulation Q tax rate,

Table 6-3. Upper Limit Estimate of Yearly Wealth Transfer Due to Interest Ceilings on Demand Deposits and Savings Accounts

	Demand Deposits ($B)	*Savings Deposits ($B)*	*Required Reserves ($B)*	*CP Rate (6-month)*	*Savings Ceilings*	*Implied Regulatory "Tax" Rate*	*Transfer ($B)*
1965	126.3	87.6	21.7	4.38	4.00	0.38	4.92
1970	153.8	93.7	28.3	7.71	4.50	3.21	12.67
1975	205.0	148.6	35.0	6.32	5.00	1.32	12.68
1980	253.9	186.0	42.9	12.29	5.25	7.04	39.12
1982 (June)	229.0	158.6	40.4	13.59	5.25	8.34	38.85

estimated here as the difference between the ceiling rate and the six-month commercial paper rate, and the total implied tax estimated as the interest income foregone by owners of demand and savings deposits.

Of the total transfer of wealth away from depositors, part accrues to the Federal Reserve and ultimately to the U.S. Treasury. This part is determined by the amount of noninterest-bearing required reserves that banks must hold associated with their deposit liabilities. One estimate of this magnitude is given by applying the commercial paper rate to the total amount of reserves. The rest of the transfer accrues to banks, although much of this, as in the fixed commission example, may be returned to depositors through nonprice competition. For example, extra free services may be offered to depositors, and free gifts may also be part of the depositors' total return.

As with fixed commission, the tax rate and total tax transfer changed dramatically. In this case, however, the change was mainly linked to higher interest rates which, in turn, reflected mainly the higher inflation under the new monetary regime. The most dramatic increase in this tax rate occurred in the late 1970s, and it induced many innovations in the money markets. Most notably, money market funds and other mechanisms that allowed depositors to reduce or avoid the increased regulatory tax grew to enormous size. In a sense, and to the extent that these funds hold bank Commercial Paper, Bankers Acceptances, etc., the funds can be viewed as intermediating between banks and their own customers. As a result, the tax base (deposits), actually declined in most of the recent period of extraordinarily high tax rates since 1980.

The part of the new monetary regime associated with high inflation and high interest rates has radically changed the wealth transfer and tax rates of the financial regulatory structure. Regulators have moved an inch in relaxing some of these regulations, and the market has moved a mile in creating innovative methods to avoid the oppressive tax, mainly by eroding the tax base—regulated deposits.

Market Responses to the New Monetary Regime

The growth in financial risk and uncertainty over the past 15 years has elicited a number of more or less predictable responses in the private sector. Much more attention than ever before is devoted to identifying and analyzing financial risk. Risk that can be diversified, at least in large portfolios, is either diversified away or at least managed more carefully and knowledgeably than before. But even after addressing diversifiable risk, usually that associated with firms, industries, or countries, there remains a residual market risk—

associated with global business cycles, for example—that is difficult or impossible to eliminate. And this risk has been large in recent years.

The development of a sophisticated financial risk market—offering financial futures and options—is another offspring of the new monetary regime. Futures and options on debt instruments and currencies have greatly reduced the costs associated with managing financial risk. They are rapidly becoming an integral part of financial management, and their use should be a permanent fixture, even if the overall level of financial risk declines during the 1980s.

Summary

Of the many factors that changed between the 1960s and 1970s, the change in domestic and international monetary regimes seems to me the most important and fundamental. If the 1960s could be characterized by low and steady inflation and more or less fixed exchange rates—with the implied coordination of national economic policies—the 1970s could be characterized by accelerating and volatile inflation and interest rates, and volatile exchange rates. Both regulation and private risk management are changing dramatically in response to the new environment, and these changes are likely to continue through the 1980s.

DISCUSSION

Donald D. Hester

When I was invited to discuss Dick Zecher's paper, I was told that it would examine the impact of financial innovations on financial markets—an exciting topic. The program lists Zecher's paper as Financial Risk Management in the 1980s—even more promising! This paper is actually entitled Financial Innovations in the 1980s. The paper is about none of these things.

It is, instead, a very general discussion of monetary growth variability in the 1970s and how such unsteady growth may have led to innovations then. Much of the paper is a diatribe against artificial interferences with free market pricing and the obsolete condition of bank regulation. Zecher illustrates his argument with two examples that are intended to measure the maximum losses that may have been inflicted because of administered pricing in the case of stock trading commissions and because of ceilings on interest rates that banks can pay on demand and savings deposits. These are hardly hot topics in the banking innovation environment of today. I know few people who will bother to defend administered prices or interest ceilings on bank deposits. There are a few passing references to money market mutual funds and to financial instrument futures markets, but no formal analysis. As everyone knows, both of these innovations occurred by the end of 1975.

Finally, there is a reference or two to options on financial instrument futures, but no discussion about how a sophisticated money market bank might make use of such opportunities.

In my comments on Zecher's paper, I plan to review some of his more stimulating ideas and then discuss aspects of innovations that bear on questions of risk exposure by households, firms, individual banks, and the banking system. My focus will be on the 1980s and, therefore, is unavoidably somewhat conjectural.

Zecher views the last fifteen years as being a period of substantial innovation in which traditional financial firms are offering a much wider range of services that greatly reduce the costs of managing financial services and risk. Perhaps he is right, but that cheery view does not seem to be consistent with substantial losses that many banks are incurring and growing leverage throughout the banking system. Bank stock prices are far below book values of net worth.

He believes that innovations were largely a consequence of the changed monetary regimes in the United States and in the world that were precipitated by the U.S. decision to abrogate the Bretton Woods Agreement. That decision by President Nixon was not made in a vacuum; it was forced by the deterioration in the U.S. balance of payments through the 1960s. In my view, Zecher's timing is off. Eurodollars, congeneric holding company conversions, and bank-related commercial paper began in about 1966. Repurchase agreements and federal credit programs surged in the late 1960s.

In Zecher's view, monetary regimes change when means and standard deviations of money growth and interest rates change, as shown in figures 6–1 and 6–2. That is a loose and slippery definition of a regime change. His interest rate figure would look very different if he had begun with 1955 instead of 1960. The second half of the 1950s was a period of extraordinary interest rate instability by his measure, but is not especially remembered for innovations. On the other hand, he apparently does not think innovations were of great importance for macro questions because he finds events in the 1970s "consistent with traditional theories that emphasize conservation of money balances as inflation and interest rates rise." I disagree with Zecher's interpretation: he fails to take account of the long period during that decade when the real federal funds rate was untypically negative and its more recent record highs. (It was also negative during the late 1950s.)

His emphasis on erratic short-run money growth as a stimulus for innovation seems peculiar, because the volatility *followed* most of the innovations. Indeed, the greatest period of volatility in figure 6–2 occurred in

1980 and 1981; those years include the effects from activating the Credit Control Act of 1969. Financial instrument futures markets had been in existence for five years by then. More importantly, until 1975, unemployment had not reached 8 percent, and fluctuations in real economic activity had been comparatively mild. It might better be asked whether recent real and nominal instability are a consequence of earlier financial market innovations.

I now want briefly to turn to the question of whether innovations have affected the risk-absorbing capacity of financial institutions and the economic system. I agree with Zecher that major changes in risk management and regulation are likely.

Soaring recent bankruptcy rates among households and corporations raise serious questions about the ability of the system to absorb shocks. Are recent innovations in mortgage loan contracts shifting risks to home purchasers which are beyond their risk-bearing capacity? Can corporate America continue to be stable and internationally competitive as the maturity of its debt and liabilities shorten? Are financial institutions failing in their responsibilities to absorb risks and to distribute risk-bearing efficiently throughout the economy? What prompts large banks to advance $4 billion to a security dealer with a net worth of $20 million, to lend $1 billion or more through a dubious agent in Oklahoma, or to advance many times their net worth to such high flyers as Brazil, Argentina and Mexico? A shortcoming of Zecher's paper is that it doesn't address these questions, which must be answered in the 1980s.

Let me suggest that futures markets are a step in the right direction, but that they fall considerably short of being a solution to the problem of growing risk. First, traders in futures traditionally and predictably do so on margin. They are, therefore, subject to margin calls. Banks and others that use futures markets to hedge, therefore, will be subject to new risks of calls and will, if anything, be on a shorter tether than heretofore. It is as if private brokers are partially replacing bank examiners. They are only partial replacements, because brokers care only about a client's margin and not about his potential insolvency. Second, the number and variety of futures markets are likely to be quite limited in the 1980s. Even today several financial instrument futures markets, such as those for commercial paper and medium-term securities, have limited volume and may not survive. Therefore, most risks can only be cross-hedged. The basis, that elegant constant that makes hedging feasible, is likely to be quite variable in most cross-hedging situations. In brief, there are a lot of cracks through which an institution may fall. Third, hedging and speculation in futures markets require a certain amount of sophistication. It may be that this expertise will develop, but I sense from studies published by the Federal Reserve Banks of Atlanta and Kansas City that banks are not interested in plunging in today.

Zecher mentions options as a second device for reallocating risk. They are attractive in one respect, because they involve no margin calls. On the other hand, studies of options almost always show that the rates of return to option purchasers are sizably negative. (I ignore the obvious tax games in this discussion.) The reason is that the risk premiums offered by option sellers are high. It seems implausible that sophisticated bankers would volunteer to pay such large premia to shed their risk exposure. It certainly does not sound as though this innovation will "greatly reduce the cost of managing financial returns and risks," as Zecher suggests. If he believes that risk premia will decline, he should argue this explicitly and formally.

A third device which he does not discuss is the seeming reinsurance feature of the Eurodollar market. I need to digress to explain what a reinsurance market is. The insurance industry has developed a secondary market in which the primary external policies for specific risks are proportionately reallocated in order to share system risk more effectively. The market has been thoroughly studied and works. It works because risks on policies are generally understood and priced meaningfully. The system cannot work in the case of banks, because for competitive reasons banks are (or should be if the Penn Square situation conveys anything) unwilling to trust each other or exchange information about risk exposure. In such situations, risks cannot be sensibly priced. Large syndications of loans are a legitimate form of risk-sharing, but that occurs in the primary market and therefore does not constitute a reinsurance market.

The seeming reinsurance feature in the Eurodollar market that I allude to is the massive volume of interbank deposits, probably about $1.2 trillion today. Why does this exist? It exists, in part, so that multinational banks understand that they must—in Ben Franklin's words—"all hang together or all hang separately." This has nothing to do with diversifying specific risks. Instead, it prevents banks from walking away from a sinking debtor quickly. It is a blood oath contract that requires banks to cooperate with one another. This innovation does not protect the public.

The welfare of the public should continue to be the concern of bank regulators in the 1980s. I refer to the safety of their deposits, the satisfaction of terms of contracts that the public arranges with banks and other regulated financial institutions, and the predictability of value of these contracts in real terms. None of the innovations mentioned focus on the welfare of the public in these senses. They focus on the welfare of financial institutions. The welfare of both financial institutions and the public can be preserved much more simply than by resorting to all these gimmicks.

The solution is for regulators rigorously to enforce a lower set of leverage ceilings and to require that banks and other regulated institutions, whose equity slips relative to their liabilities, promptly restore their ratios. Through this mechanism, the negative externalities to the public that are associated with wanton risk-taking by regulated financial institutions will be internalized. Financial institutions will have a stronger incentive to act as responsible fiduciaries.

Finally, there is a transitional problem in going from the present unsettled conditions to a world of adequate capitalization. During this period, the creditors of banks and other regulated institutions must be protected, if necessary, at the expense of stockholders. This is the challenge to regulators in the 1980s.

IV LUNCHEON SPEECH

7 AN INSIDER'S VIEW OF INNOVATIONS AND MONETARY POLICYMAKING

Lawrence K. Roos

It is a pleasure to welcome all of you to the Federal Reserve Bank of St. Louis. It is a privilege, as well, to have the opportunity of joining you in considering what I believe to be one of the most important, as well as most controversial, issues currently facing monetary policymakers—namely, the impact financial innovations have on financial markets and on the relationship between monetary aggregates and the economy.

Assertions by some that financial innovations have made monetary targeting obsolete have set off a frenzied search for alternative policy targets and approaches. Legislation has been introduced in Congress that would require the Federal Reserve to target on some measure of interest rates; academicians have offered a variety of other possibilities, ranging from the monetary base to the broadest of credit aggregates. Even Federal Reserve officials themselves have entered the fray, openly airing their differences of opinion in the pages of the *Wall Street Journal*, their respective *Reviews*, and a variety of other publications.

Conferences such as this that provide an opportunity for sober (I trust) discussion of fundamental issues can be extremely helpful to policymakers. First, they serve as a means for clearing away the more irrelevant aspects of the subject matter and for bringing to the foreground the key issues involved.

By sweeping away the clutter, they often separate real issues from pseudo ones.

Second, they usually generate the lastest empirical evidence relating both to problems and to suggested solutions. By so doing, they provide policymakers with information that, given the usual publishing lags, might otherwise not be available for several months or years.

Then, too, in attending conferences such as this, it is possible to judge, by observing the extent of the disagreements, disputes, and debates among participants, whether there really are substantive differences of opinion and analysis among the experts. When ancient mapmakers disagreed about what dangers lay in unexplored territory, they labeled those parts of their maps with the warning "Dragons live here." Policymakers too need to know where dragons are lurking.

Finally, on rare occasions, answers to specific issues or problems actually emerge at conferences. When this occurs, it can be counted on to produce a state of nirvana in policymakers. At least that's what I've been told; it has never actually happened at one that I've attended—at least, up to now.

While I really don't expect to achieve nirvana at this conference, I am here to observe and to learn, from the papers and discussions, how much you believe that financial innovations have affected monetary policy and financial markets. Your conclusions will be of value, even if you haven't been able to uncover all the answers by noon tomorrow. Given the policymaking process, every bit of available information helps. With the time constraints policymakers face, we cannot always wait until the definitive study has been completed, the final regression has been run, and the ultimate Nobel Prize for Economics has been awarded. We must make decisions now, using our best judgment about the relationships between instruments, targets, and goals—realizing, at the same time, that the world is an uncertain place and that truth is a highly elusive commodity.

Now, you are probably wondering why I am up here giving this luncheon talk. I assure you that it is not because Ted Balbach knows, from long experience, that when three or more people are gathered together to give speeches at the St. Louis Federal Reserve, all hell breaks loose if Roos isn't on the program. That's not so. It's rather that I believe it might put the policy aspects of the problem in perspective if you know how at least one policymaker views the issue.

In approaching policy decisions, I have always felt that policymakers should have some consistent framework of analysis to guide their decisions. Otherwise they are likely to suffer the same fate as a captain whose ship is adrift in a fog-shrouded ocean without compass or other navigational aid.

Three years ago, at a conference similar to this one at this bank, I described several concepts or navigational aids that I find useful in assessing the consequences of monetary policy actions on the economy. Briefly stated, they are that: (1) inflation is fundamentally a monetary phenomenon; (2) abrupt and substantial changes in the growth of money, if sufficiently prolonged, have dramatic and usually unfortunate consequences for the economy; and (3) the growth of money can best be controlled by controlling the growth of the monetary base.

Now, despite what you may have heard to the contrary, these are not necessarily viewed by the St. Louis Federal Reserve as the "Three Commandments of Monetary Policy." Nor do we think of them as "The Gospel according to St. Louis," even though a fair amount of the research done over the years supporting their validity has been done at this bank. I view these concepts only as a frame of reference in arriving at decisions. It is this framework that has influenced my initial point of view concerning the impact of innovation on monetary policy, and I would like to offer a few tentative speculations on the impact of innovations in light of these concepts.

First, I have not found that recent innovations have had a noticeable impact on the relationship of trend money growth to inflation. Prior to the end of 1979, both trend money growth and inflation were clearly accelerating. In part, this pattern was responsible for the Federal Reserve's October 6, 1979 policy change. Since October 1979, there has been a marked decline in the trend rate of growth in M1, and rates of inflation have slowed considerably as well. It even appears that the relationship between the measured rate of inflation and trend M1 growth has narrowed. I will certainly admit that this observation is based on a very simple comparison and that full investigation requires extensive statistical and econometric analysis. Still, the simple comparison does not suggest that there is a problem in continued use of the relationship of trend money growth and inflation for policy purposes.

Now, what about the second concept—that excessively erratic short-run money growth can produce short-run swings in real economic activity? At least at first glance, short-run monetary impulses seem to have had essentially the same impact on the economy in recent years as they did previously. For example, as many of you know, we have had several short-run periods of widely diverse money growth. In particular, from November 1979 to May 1980 and from April 1981 to October 1981, we had two extended periods when M1 growth was essentially zero. In both cases, these protracted slowdowns in M1 growth were associated with sharp reductions in nominal GNP growth and declines in real GNP.

Again, this comparison is just a simple juxtaposition of short-run money growth and movements in real economic activity—not a sophisticated and detailed analysis. But, once again, the comparison points out something that I find interesting—namely, that the expected happened! Real output growth declined significantly when there were sizable reductions in money growth that persisted for more than six months. Strangely enough for those who argue that the world has changed, the second concept still seems to possess some validity.

Also, the third concept—that the growth of money is closely related to the growth of the monetary base—seems to be surviving as well. Since the fourth quarter of 1979, the monetary base and M1 have grown at average annual rates of 7 percent and 6.3 percent, respectively. Not only are both rates of growth down sharply from what they were over the prior four years, it turns out that the reduction in money growth is virtually identical to the drop in the growth of the adjusted monetary base. As far as I can tell, a similar, though somewhat noisier, relationship still continues to exist between short-run base growth and short-run money growth.

Thus, after viewing what has occurred since 1979, albeit in a simple fashion, I am hard pressed to find any convincing evidence that financial innovations have had significant impacts either on the relationship between monetary base and money growth or on the relationship between measures of monetary impulses and the economy. Since this impression conflicts directly with those of others, I must conclude either that I have somehow overlooked some important evidence or that, at least for the present, the impressions of others who feel differently about the effect of innovations are in error.

This puzzle is one that I hope will be resolved by the papers and discussions at this conference. As I see it, if financial innovations have significantly distorted the relationships between monetary base growth, money growth, and the economy, then some of the concepts that have helped me to make policy decisions in the past are no longer valid.

If, on the other hand, these relationships have been essentially unaffected by innovations that have occurred over the past several years, then they still provide useful information to guide policy actions. If this is indeed the case, then the recent financial innovations can be ignored by policymakers until such time as they do, in fact, affect policy outcomes.

I would like, once again, to welcome you to St. Louis and to this bank. I appreciate your willingness to spend one-and-a-half days trying to solve a problem that plagues and puzzles so many people. And, to demonstrate my appreciation, I promise to remain attentive and interested, even when Dick Porter starts discussing divisia aggregation and the error pattern from double-logarithmic money-demand estimation. I sincerely hope that your stay in St. Louis will be at least as enjoyable as that promises to be.

CONFERENCE PARTICIPANTS

Rachel Balbach
Centerre Bank

Anatol B. Balbach
Federal Reserve Bank of St. Louis

Dallas S. Batten
Federal Reserve Bank of St. Louis

Scott Bloom
University of Missouri-Columbia

Mike Bordo
University of South Carolina

Norman N. Bowsher
Federal Reserve Bank of St. Louis

Daniel P. Brennan
Federal Reserve Bank of St. Louis

Donald M. Brown
Federal Reserve Bank of St. Louis

Ruth A. Bryant
Federal Reserve Bank of St. Louis

Albert E. Burger
Federal Reserve Bank of St. Louis

Claudia Campbell
Washington University

John B. Carlson
Federal Reserve Bank of Cleveland

Keith M. Carlson
Federal Reserve Bank of St. Louis

Dan Clark
Centerre Bank

Lindley Clark
Wall Street Journal

William Cox
Federal Reserve Bank of Atlanta

William Cullison
Federal Reserve Bank of Richmond

Larry Davidson
Indiana University

Harold Demsetz
Washington University

William Dewald
Ohio State University

Betty Dickhaus
University of Missouri-Columbia

Steve Fazzari
Washington University

William Foy
Buckmaster and Moore

Joel Fried
Federal Reserve Bank of St. Louis

William T. Gavin
Federal Reserve Bank of Cleveland

R. Alton Gilbert
Federal Reserve Bank of St. Louis

Joe Golec
Washington University

Kevin Grier
Washington University

Bruce Halliday
Fontbonne College

Michael J. Hamburger
Office of Management and Budget

Scott E. Hein
Federal Reserve Bank of St. Louis

Donald D. Hester
University of Wisconsin

Jerome Hollenhorst
Southern Illinois University

Linda C. Hoops
Federal Reserve Bank of St. Louis

Lee Hoskins
Pittsburgh National Bank

Homer Jones
Federal Reserve Bank of St. Louis

Jerry L. Jordan
Anderson Schools of Management

Edward J. Kane
Ohio State University

Denis Karnosky
Department of the Treasury

Bob Keleher
Federal Reserve Bank of Atlanta

Michael Keran
Federal Reserve Bank of San Francisco

Sandy Krieger
Federal Reserve Bank of New York

Jan Loeys
Federal Reserve Bank of Philadelphia

Joseph McKenna
University of Missouri-St. Louis

Kevin Maloney
Washington University

Steve Mann
University of Missouri-Columbia

Paul Merz
St. Louis University

Laurence H. Meyer
Washington University

Hyman P. Minsky
Washington University

Michael Nelson
Illinois State University

Mack Ott
Federal Reserve Bank of St. Louis

Seymour Patterson
Northeast Missouri State University

Mick Pirchett
University of Missouri-Columbia

Richard Porter
Federal Reserve Board

David Ramsey
Illinois State University

Robert Rasche
Michigan State University

David Resler
First National Bank of Chicago

John Roger
University of Missouri-Columbia

Lawrence K. Roos
Federal Reserve Bank of St. Louis

Harvey Rosenblum
Federal Reserve Bank of Chicago

Gary J. Santoni
Federal Reserve Bank of St. Louis

Karl Scheld
Federal Reserve Bank of Chicago

Frank Steindl
Oklahoma State University

Gary Stern
Federal Reserve Bank of Minneapolis

Neil A. Stevens
Federal Reserve Bank of St. Louis

Courtenay C. Stone
Federal Reserve Bank of St. Louis

Werner Sublette
Northeast Missouri State University

John A. Tatom
Federal Reserve Bank of St.Louis

Daniel L. Thornton
Federal Reserve Bank of St. Louis

Michael E. Trebing
Federal Reserve Bank of St. Louis

Chris Varvares
Washington University

Marcia Wallace
Washington University

Eric Webber
Federal Reserve Bank of St. Louis

Ben Weberman
Forbes

Charles Webster
Federal Reserve Bank of Kansas City

Patrick Welch
St. Louis University

Jai Hoon Yang
Morgan Guaranty Trust Co.

J. Richard Zecher
Chase-Manhattan Bank

MIX
Papier aus verantwortungsvollen Quellen
Paper from responsible sources
FSC® C105338

If you have any concerns about our products,
you can contact us on
ProductSafety@springernature.com

In case Publisher is established outside the EU,
the EU authorized representative is:
Springer Nature Customer Service Center GmbH
Europaplatz 3, 69115 Heidelberg, Germany

Printed by Libri Plureos GmbH
in Hamburg, Germany